Pearl of Wisdom

Buddhist Prayers and Practices

Book I

compiled by Bhikshuni Thubten Chodron

First edition 1988
Sixth edition (revised) 2011

For further information, contact:
Sravasti Abbey
692 Country Lane, Newport WA 99156, USA
Email: office.sravasti@gmail.com
http://www.sravasti.org

For audio and video Dharma talks, see:
http://www.thubtenchodron.org
http://www.youtube.com/sravastiabbey
http://sravasti.org/programs/internet.html

To hear melodies for chanting verses and texts go to:
http://www.thubtenchodron.org/PrayersAndPractices/index.html

Other books by Ven. Thubten Chodron:
Buddhism for Beginners (Snow Lion Publications)
Cultivating a Compassionate Heart: The Yoga Method of Chenrezig (Snow Lion Publications)
Guided Meditations on the Stages of the Path (Snow Lion Publications)
How to Free Your Mind: Tara the Liberator (Snow Lion Publications)
Open Heart, Clear Mind (Snow Lion Publications)
The Path to Happiness (Texas Buddhist Association)
Taming the Mind (Snow Lion Publications)
Working with Anger (Snow Lion Publications)

© Sravasti Abbey
ISBN 981-00-0558-X
Cover design by Jonathan Owen and Ven. Thubten Jigme

This book is printed on 30% post-consumer waste (recycled) paper.

Pearl of Wisdom

Buddhist Prayers and Practices

Book I

Table of Contents

Introduction

Many people question, "What are the meaning and purpose of reciting spiritual verses and following guided meditations?" Recitation, guided meditations, and chanting are not merely moving the mouth; they are moving the mind. They are ways of guiding our thoughts and energy in a certain direction; they are a technique to help us transform our mind. By contemplating the meaning of what we are saying or reading, we make the prayers and practices effective in enriching the quality of our life.

Building up good habits of the mind is a gradual process that takes time. We do the same practices and recitations each day in order to train and familiarize ourselves with a new way of regarding and relating to ourselves and others.

But why do practices and say verses written by other people? Why not do our own? The great masters have realized the path to awakening, and the practices and verses they have written from their own experience show us the correct way to train our mind so that we can develop those same realizations. As we become familiar with the Buddha's teachings, we may say prayers from our heart that express the same meaning in our own words.

Regarding formal Dharma practice as completely distinct from daily life is a deterrent to our progress. Setting aside a quiet time for practice each day helps us concentrate on transforming our disturbing emotions and incorrect attitudes into beneficial ones. But our daily life with all its activities is the testing ground that shows us which qualities are firm within us and which ones still need to be developed. For the mindful person who is dedicated to developing his or her Buddha potential, formal meditation, recitation of verses, and the activities of daily life complement each other.

Explanation from a teacher is most helpful to understand the meaning of the verses and practices and how to think when we do them. Thus I strongly recommend that you attend teachings from a qualified spiritual mentor. In the meantime, a short overview of the practices and recitations in this book will help you know how to use them.

Before and after we listen to Dharma teachings, we prepare our mind by paying homage to the Buddha, reciting the "Heart Sutra," purifying interferences, paying homage to Manjushri the Buddha of Wisdom, offering the mandala (our universe), taking refuge and generating bodhicitta (the altruistic intention). This does not mean that these cannot be recited and contemplated on at other times – they can be done whenever you wish and they will help you to settle your mind.

The "Meditation on the Buddha" is a wonderful practice to do daily. Towards the end of this practice, contemplate the stages of the path to awakening. This may be done by reciting and contemplating any of the brief texts that follow. If you are short on time, you can also do the "Abbreviated Recitations Before Meditation," recite one of the brief texts, and then contemplate a specific topic from the stages of the path.

"The Extensive Offering Practice" is done to create great merit by making offerings to sentient beings and holy beings. This practice reduces attachment and cultivates delight in giving. "Evening Chants" are Chinese Buddhist practices that are excellent for purifying and concentrating the mind. Since our mind is overcome by disturbing emotions on a daily basis, "Purification Practices" are good to do each evening. In that way we clean up our actions regarding the day's events so we can have a good rest and wake up refreshed. To dedicate the merit we and others create in the past, present, and future, we recite and contemplate any or all of the dedication verses. We also recite long life prayers for our spiritual mentors at the end of the day.

Since we eat and drink frequently throughout the day, offering our food to the Three Jewels is an excellent way to create merit. Lunch is the main meal at monasteries, so the full offering – the five contemplations and all the offering verses before eating – are chanted then. For breakfast and medicine meal (dinner), the last three verses are sufficient. After lunch we offer a bit of the leftovers to the pretas (hungry ghosts) and then dedicate for all the beings involved in us receiving our meal.

"Verses for Various Occasions" are short verses that help us transform ordinary activities into the path. "The Eight Mahayana Precepts" is a wonderful practice to do on new and full moon days or on any day when we want to rejuvenate our practice. "Taking Refuge and Precepts" is a ceremony for lay practitioners to do to renew their precepts. It is recommended to do this twice a month – on new and full moon days if possible, but other days are also fine. It is also good to review the "Guidelines for the Practice of Refuge" at this time.

"The Six Preparatory Practices" details how to prepare for meditation sessions, and "Practicing Dharma in Daily Life" sets the framework for our entire practice by describing what to think when we wake up, eat, engage with sense objects, make offerings, go to work, bathe, and prepare for bed. You may want to read this first because it puts the other practices in this book in context.

The consecration ritual is used to invite the Buddhas to abide in a new statue, painting, or stupa. "Praise of the Teacher, the Buddha, Through His Twelve Deeds" is more devotional, evoking appreciation and respect for our Teacher.

A good companion book for *Pearl of Wisdom* is *Guided Meditations on the Stages of the Path*. It contains explanations on setting up a daily practice, the various types of meditation, counteracting distractions, and working with afflictions. It also has an extensive outline and an audio CD that will help you do the meditations on the stages of the path to awakening.

Many thanks to those who helped in the preparation of this book. First and foremost, gratitude is due to the Buddha, the lineages of spiritual mentors, and my own spiritual mentors, especially His Holiness the Dalai Lama, Tsenzhab Serkong Rinpoche, Lama Yeshe and Zopa Rinpoche. Also, many thanks to all those who translated the prayers and practices, to Thubten Dekyong for checking the translations, and to all those who helped in the publication of this book. All errors are due to my own ignorance and carelessness.

Bhikshuni Thubten Chodron
Sravasti Abbey, 2011

Recitations Before and After Teachings

Homage to Shakyamuni Buddha

To the teacher, endowed transcendent destroyer, one thus gone, foe destroyer, completely and fully awakened one, perfect in knowledge and good conduct, one gone to bliss, knower of the world, supreme guide of beings to be tamed, teacher of gods and humans, to you the Buddha, endowed transcendent destroyer, glorious conqueror Shakyamuni, I prostrate, make offerings and go for refuge. (3x)

When, O supreme among humans, you were born on this earth,
You paced seven strides,
Then said, "I am supreme in this world."
To you, who were wise then, I bow.

With pure bodies, form supremely fine;
Wisdom ocean, like a golden mountain;
Fame that blazes in the three worlds,
Winner of the best – supreme guide, to you I bow.

With the supreme signs, face like the spotless moon,
Color like gold – to you I bow.
You are immaculate, the three worlds are not.
Incomparable wise one – to you I bow.

Great compassionate Protector,
All-knowing Teacher,
Field of merit and good qualities vast as an ocean –
To the Tathagata, I bow.

Through purity, freeing from attachment,
Through virtue, freeing from the lower realms,
Unique, supreme ultimate reality –
To the Dharma that is peace, I bow.

Having freed themselves, showing the path to freedom too,
Well established in the trainings,
The holy field endowed with good qualities –
To the Sangha, I bow.

Do not commit any non-virtuous actions,
Perform only perfect virtuous actions,
Subdue your mind completely –
This is the teaching of the Buddha.

A star, a mirage, a flame of a lamp,
An illusion, a drop of dew, a bubble,
A dream, a flash of lightning, a cloud –
See conditioned things as such!

Through this merit may sentient beings
Attain the state of all-seeing, subdue the foe of faults,
And be delivered from the ocean of cyclic existence,
Perturbed by the waves of ageing, sickness, and death.

Heart of Wisdom Sutra

Thus I have heard: at one time, the Blessed One was dwelling in Rajagriha on Vultures Mountain together in one method with a great assembly of monastics and a great assembly of bodhisattvas. At that time, the Blessed One was absorbed in the concentration of the countless aspects of phenomena called Profound Illumination.

At that time also Superior Avalokiteshvara, the bodhisattva, the great being, was looking perfectly at the practice of the profound perfection of wisdom, perfectly looking at the emptiness of inherent existence of the five aggregates also.

Then, through the power of Buddha, Venerable Shariputra said to Superior Avalokiteshvara, the bodhisattva, the great being, "How should a child of the lineage train who wishes to engage in the practice of the profound perfection of wisdom?"

Thus he spoke, and Superior Avalokiteshvara, the bodhisattva, the great being, replied to Venerable Shariputra as follows:

"Shariputra, whatever son or daughter of the lineage wishes to engage in the practice of the profound perfection of wisdom should look perfectly like this: subsequently looking perfectly and correctly at the emptiness of inherent existence of the five aggregates also.

"Form is empty; emptiness is form. Emptiness is not other than form; form also is not other than emptiness. Likewise, feeling, discrimination, compositional factors and consciousness are empty.

"Shariputra, like this all phenomena are merely empty, having no characteristics. They are not produced and do not cease. They have no defilement and no separation from defilement. They have no decrease and no increase.

"Therefore, Shariputra, in emptiness there is no form, no feeling, no discrimination, no compositional factors, no consciousness. There is no eye, no ear, no nose, no tongue, no body, no mind; no form, no sound, no smell, no taste, no tactile object, no phenomenon. There is no eye element and so forth up to no mind element and also up to no element of mental consciousness. There is no ignorance and no exhaustion of ignorance, and so forth up to no ageing and death and no exhaustion of ageing and death. Likewise, there is no suffering, origin, cessation or path; no exalted wisdom, no attainment and also no non-attainment.

"Therefore Shariputra, because there is no attainment, bodhisattvas rely on and abide in the perfection of wisdom; their minds have no obstructions and no fear. Passing utterly beyond perversity, they attain the final state beyond sorrow. Also, all the Buddhas who perfectly reside in the three times, relying upon the perfection of wisdom, become manifest and complete Buddhas in the state of unsurpassed, perfect and complete awakening.

"Therefore, the mantra of the perfection of wisdom, the mantra of great knowledge, the unsurpassed mantra, the equal-to-the-unequalled mantra, the mantra that thoroughly pacifies all suffering, since it is not false, should be known as the truth. The mantra of the perfection of wisdom is proclaimed:

tayata gate gate paragate parasamgate bodhi soha

(Gone, gone, gone beyond, gone completely beyond, awakened, so be it!)

"Shariputra, a bodhisattva, a great being, should train in the profound perfection of wisdom like this."

Then the Blessed One arose from that concentration and said to Superior Avalokiteshvara, the bodhisattva, the great being, that he had spoken well. "Good, good, O child of the lineage. It is like that. Since it is like that, just as you have revealed, the profound perfection of wisdom should be practiced in that way, and the tathagatas will also rejoice."

When the Blessed One had said this, Venerable Shariputra, Superior Avalokiteshvara, the bodhisattva, the great being, and that entire assembly of disciples as well as the worldly beings – gods, humans, demi-gods and spirits – were delighted and highly praised what had been spoken by the Blessed One.

Purifying Interferences

To those from the pure and supreme places who enjoy space (emptiness),
Who possess the five superknowledges and can magically emanate,
Care for us practitioners, like a mother for her child.
I prostrate to the assembly of dakinis of the three places.

ah ka samara tsasha dara samaraya phat (recite several times)

tayata gate gate paragate parasamgate bodhi soha

By the truth of the existence of the Three Jewels, may all inner and outer hindrances and adversities be overcome! (clap)
May they become non-existent! (clap)
May they be pacified! (clap)
May all destructive forces opposed to the Dharma be completely pacified!

May the eighty thousand obstacles be pacified. May we be separated from all adverse conditions and may we obtain conducive circumstances and everything good. May there be auspiciousness, happiness, and well-being, here, right now!

Manjushri

Homage to Manjushri,
the Buddha of Wisdom

Obeisance to my Guru and Protector, Manjushri,
Who holds to his heart a scriptural text symbolic of his seeing all
things as they are,
Whose intelligence shines forth like the sun, unclouded by the two
obscurations,
Who teaches in sixty ways, with the loving compassion of a parent
for his only child, all wanderers caught in the prison of samsara,
confused in the darkness of their ignorance, overwhelmed by their
suffering.
You, whose dragon-thunder-like proclamation of Dharma arouses
us from the stupor of our delusions and frees us from the iron
chains of our karma;
Who wields the sword of wisdom hewing down suffering wherever
its sprouts appear, clearing away the darkness of ignorance;
You, whose princely body is adorned with the one hundred and
twelve marks of a Buddha,
Who has completed the stages achieving the highest perfection of a
bodhisattva,
Who has been pure from the beginning,
I bow down to you, O Manjushri;

om ah ra pa tsa na dhi (recite many times)

With the brilliance of your wisdom, O compassionate one,
Illuminate the darkness enclosing my mind,
Awaken my intelligence and wisdom
So that I may gain insight into the Buddha's words and the texts
that explain them.

Mandala Offering, Refuge and Bodhicitta

OM vajra ground AH HUM, mighty golden ground. OM vajra fence AH HUM, the iron fence around the edge, In the center is Mount Meru, the king of mountains, in the east the continent Videha, in the south Jambudvipa, in the west Godaniya, in the north Kuru. In the east are the sub-continents Deha and Videha, in the south Camara and Aparacamara, in the west Shatha and Uttaramantrina, in the north Kurava and Kaurava. Here are the precious mountain, wish-granting tree, wish-fulfilling cow, unploughed harvest.

Here are the precious wheel, precious jewel, precious queen, precious minister, precious elephant, precious horse, precious general, great treasure vase. Here are the goddess of beauty, goddess of garlands, goddess of song, goddess of dance, goddess of flowers, goddess of incense, goddess of light, goddess of perfume. Here are the sun, moon, precious parasol, and victory banner. In the center are the marvelous riches of gods and humans, with nothing missing, pure and delightful. I offer these as a Buddha-field to my glorious, holy, kind root guru, the lineage gurus, and

in particular to the master of the entire doctrine, the noble spiritual mentor, as an offering while requesting profound Mahayana instructions. (before teachings, to request them)

in particular to the master of the entire doctrine, the noble spiritual mentor, as an offering to thank you for your kindness because we have received the profound Mahayana teachings. (after teachings, in appreciation for having received teachings)

to the great Je Tsongkhapa, Buddha who is the King of Sages, Vajradhara, and the entire assembly of deities, (in general, before meditation)

Please accept these with compassion for the sake of migrating beings. Having accepted them, please bestow on me and on the mother sentient beings abiding as far as the limits of space your inspiration with loving compassion.

Short Mandala Offering

This ground, anointed with perfume, flowers strewn,
Mount Meru, four lands, sun and moon,
Imagined as a Buddha land and offered to you
May all beings enjoy this pure land.

Mandala Offering to Request Teachings

Venerable holy gurus, in the space of your truth body, from billowing clouds of your wisdom and love, let fall the rain of the profound and extensive Dharma in whatever form is suitable for subduing sentient beings.

Mandala Offering after Teachings

May the spiritual teachers who lead me on the sacred path and all spiritual friends who practice it have long life. May I pacify completely all outer and inner hindrances – grant such inspiration, I pray.

May the lives of the venerable spiritual mentors be stable, and their divine actions spread in the ten directions. May the light of Lobsang's teaching, dispelling the darkness of the beings in the three worlds, always increase.

Inner Mandala Offering

The objects of attachment, aversion and ignorance – friends, enemies and strangers, my body, wealth and enjoyments – I offer these without any sense of loss. Please accept them with pleasure and inspire[1] me and others to be free from the three poisonous attitudes.

Idam guru ratna mandala kam nirya tayami

Refuge and Bodhicitta[2]

I take refuge until I have awakened in the Buddhas, the Dharma, and the Sangha. By the merit I create by listening to the Dharma, may I attain Buddhahood in order to benefit all sentient beings. (3x)

Mandala Offering and Refuge – Tibetan

om vajra bhumi ah hum, wang chen ser gyi sa zhi/ om vajra rekhe ah hum chi chag ri kor yug gi kor way u su/ ri gyal po ri rab/ shar lu pag po/ lho dzam bu ling/ nup ba lang cho/ jang dra mi nyan/ lu dang lu pag/ nga yap dang nga yap zhan/ yo dan dang lam chog dro/ dra mi nyan dang dra mi nyan gyi da/ rin po che ri wo/ pag sam gyi shing/ do joi ba/ ma mo pa yi lo tog/

kor lo rin po che/ nor bu rin po che/ tsun mo rin po che/ long po rin po che/ lang po rin po che/ ta chog rin po che/ mag pon rin po che/ ter chen poi bum pa/ / gek ma/ treng wa ma/ lu ma/ gar ma/ may tog ma/ dug po ma/ nang sal ma/ dri chap ma/ / nyi ma/ / da wa/ rin po che dug/ chog la nam par gyal way gyal tsan/ u su lha dang mi pal jor pun sum tsog pa ma tsang wa may pa/ tzang zhing

yi du wong wa di dag drin chen tza wa dang gyu par che pay pal
dan la ma dam pa nam dang/

**kye par du yang yong dzog ten pay nga dag palden lama dam
pay zhal nga ne teg pa chen po sung cho zab mo zhu way yon
du/** (before teachings, to request them)

**kye par du yang yong dzog ten pay nga dag palden lama dam
pay zhal nga ne teg pa chen po sung cho zab mo leg par tob
pay ka drin tang rak ki yon du** (after teachings, in appreciation
for having received teachings)

**kye par du yang la ma lo zang tub wang dor je chang, chen po
lha tsog kor dang che pa nam la** (in general, before meditation)

zhing kam bul war gyio/ tug je dro way don du zhe su sol/ zhe nay
kyang dog sog dro wa mar gyur nam kay ta dang nyam pay sem
chen tam che la tug tze wa chen poi go ne jin gyi lab tu sol/

Short Mandala Offering

sa zhi po kyi jug shing may tog tram
ri rab ling zhi nyi day gyan pa di
sang gye zhing du mig tay ul war gyi
dro kun nam dag zhing la cho par shog

Mandala Offering to Request Teachings

je tsun la ma dam pa kye nam kyi
cho ku ka la kyen tse drin trig nay
ji tar tsam pay dul je zim ma la
zab gye cho ki char pa ab tu sol

Mandala Offering After Teachings

day tar lam zang ton pay shey nyen dang
tsul zhin drub pay drog nam zhab ten ching
chi dang nang gi bar du cho pay tsog
nye war shi war jin gyi lab tu sol

je tsun la may ku tse ra ten ching
nam kar trin lay chog tu gye pa dang
lo zang ten pa dro may sa sum gi
dro way mun sel tag tu nay gyur chig

Inner Mandala Offering

dag gi chag dang mong sum kye pay yul
dra nyen bar sum lu dang long cho che
pang pa may par bul gyi leg zhe nay
dug sum rang sar drol war jin gyi lob

idam guru ratna mandala kam nirya tayami

Refuge and Bodhicitta

sang gye cho dang tsog kyi chog nam la
jang chub bar du dag ni kyab su chi
dag gi cho nyen gyi pay so nam kyi
drol la pan chir sang gye drub par shog (3x)

Shakyamuni Buddha

Meditation on the Buddha

Begin by observing your breath for a few minutes to calm the mind.

Think of the qualities of infinite love, compassion, wisdom, skillful means, and other wonderful qualities you aspire to develop. What would it feel like to be those qualities? Get a sense of the expansiveness and peace of having a wise and kind heart that reaches out impartially to work for the benefit of all beings.

Those qualities of love, compassion, wisdom, skillful means, and so on now appear in the physical form of the Buddha, in the space in front of you. He sits on a throne, above which is an open lotus flower, and cushions of the sun and moon disks.[3] His body is made of radiant, transparent light, as is the entire visualization. His body is golden and he wears the robes of a monastic. His right palm rests on his right knee and his left is in his lap, holding a bowl of nectar,[4] which is medicine to cure our afflictions and other hindrances. The Buddha's face is very beautiful. His smiling, compassionate gaze looks at you with total acceptance and simultaneously encompasses all sentient beings. His eyes are long, narrow, and peaceful. His lips are red and his earlobes long.

Rays of light emanate from each pore of the Buddha's body[5] and reach every part of the universe. These rays carry countless miniature Buddhas, some going out to help beings, others dissolving back into the Buddha after having finished their work.

The Buddha is surrounded by the entire lineage of spiritual teachers, all meditational deities, innumerable other Buddhas, bodhisattvas, arhats, dakas, dakinis, and Dharma protectors. To the side of each spiritual mentor is an elegant table upon which are arranged volumes of Dharma teachings.

Surrounding you are all sentient beings appearing in human form, with your mother on your left and your father on your right. The people you do not get along with are in front of you. All of you are looking at the Buddha for guidance.

Refuge and Bodhicitta

To cultivate a sense of refuge, first think of the dangers of cyclic existence by remembering your own lack of security, dissatisfaction, and suffering. Then think of all other sentient beings who, like you, flounder in cyclic existence, and generate compassion for them. Finally, think of the wonderful qualities of the Buddhas, Dharma, and Sangha, and generate confidence in their ability to guide you from the constantly recurring problems of cyclic existence. Since it's possible on the basis of your present life and mind to free yourself from all these undesirable experiences, resolve to explore that possibility to its fullest. Feel great trust and confidence in the Three Jewels and open your heart to rely on them to guide you and others from the torments of cyclic existence to the peace of liberation and awakening.

As you take refuge, imagine leading all the sentient beings around you in going for refuge to the Three Jewels. Visualize radiant light flowing from the spiritual mentors, Buddhas, bodhisattvas, and other holy beings into you and into all the beings around you, completely purifying all destructive karmic imprints and afflictions. The light also enriches you with all the wondrous qualities and realizations of the path.

Namo Gurubhya.
Namo Buddhaya.
Namo Dharmaya.
Namo Sanghaya. (3x or 7x)

Feel that you and all others have come under the protection of the Three Jewels.

Now turn your thoughts to others and contemplate how much we depend on them for everything we enjoy and know in our lives. Our food, clothing, and everything we use and enjoy come due to their efforts. Similarly, our knowledge, talents, and good qualities have been developed due to the kindness of others. Even our ability to practice the Dharma and gain realizations depends on the kindness of sentient beings.

Just as your innermost wish is to be free from suffering and to abide in happiness, so too is it the aspiration of all other beings. But, they, like you, encounter sufferings and problems in their lives, and often their difficulties are much worse than your own.

Examine your capacity to help them. At this time your ability to help them is quite limited, but if you reduce your own ignorance, anger, attachment, and other faults, and increase your good qualities such as generosity, fortitude, loving-kindness, compassion, and wisdom, you will be of greater benefit. If you become a fully awakened Buddha, you will be of the greatest possible benefit to all beings. Thus generate the altruistic intention to become a Buddha in order to benefit all sentient beings most effectively. As you recite the refuge and bodhicitta prayer, much light flows from the Buddhas and other holy beings into you and all other sentient beings around you, purifying and enriching your minds.

I take refuge until I have awakened in the Buddhas, the Dharma, and the Sangha. By the merit I create by engaging in generosity and the other far-reaching practices, may I attain Buddhahood in order to benefit all sentient beings. (3x)

The Buddha is extremely pleased with your altruistic intention. A replica emerges from him and goes to the crown of your head. He melts into golden, radiant light that flows into you, and you and the Buddha become inseparable. Feel close to the Buddha, and feel that your mind has been inspired and transformed.

Let go of all conceptions you have about yourself, particularly any self-denigrating thoughts and the concept of inherent existence, and meditate on emptiness. (Meditate)

At your heart appears a small Buddha made of light. He radiates the light of wisdom and compassion in all directions, throughout the entire universe. The light transforms all sentient beings into Buddhas and transforms all environments into pure lands – places with all conducive circumstances for practicing the Dharma and generating realizations of the path. (Meditate)

You have transformed all sentient beings and their environments into awakened beings and pure lands in your imagination. Why hasn't this become a reality? Because we sentient beings have bias and prejudice, and lack love, compassion, and joy. Wishing yourself and others to have these, contemplate the four immeasurables. Reinforce your feelings of love, compassion, joy, and equanimity for everyone – friends, relatives, strangers, as well as those who you dislike, mistrust, disapprove of, and those who have harmed you in the past.

May all sentient beings have happiness and its causes.

May all sentient beings be free of suffering and its causes.
May all sentient beings not be separated from sorrowless bliss.
May all sentient beings abide in equanimity, free of bias,
attachment, and anger.

Seven-limb Prayer

Now offer the seven-limb prayer to purify negativities and create merit.

Reverently I prostrate with my body, speech, and mind,

Imagine you and sentient beings throughout infinite space bow to the field of merit.

And present clouds of every type of offering, actual and mentally transformed.

Imagine every beautiful object you can and offer it to the field of merit. Imagine the sky filled with lovely offerings, and offer them. Similarly, think of everything and everyone to whom you are attached, and offer them to the field of merit as well.

I confess all my destructive actions accumulated since beginningless time,

Acknowledge your past mistakes and harmful actions and purify them by contemplating the four opponent powers: 1) regret, 2) taking refuge and generating bodhicitta, 3) determining not to do them again, and 4) engaging in a remedial action.

And rejoice in the virtues of all holy and ordinary beings.

Think of the virtues of all the holy and ordinary beings and feel happy. Abandon any feeling of jealousy or envy and rejoice in all the goodness in the world.

Please remain until cyclic existence ends,

Offer a double dorje, symbolizing long life, to the field of merit, and request them to live long and always be part of your life.

And turn the wheel of Dharma for sentient beings.

Offer a thousand-spoked Dharma wheel to the field of merit, requesting them to teach the Dharma and to guide you in your practice.

I dedicate all the virtues of myself and others to the great awakening.

Rejoicing at your own and others' merit, dedicate it to the awakening of yourself and all sentient beings.

Mandala Offering

With the wish to offer everything in the universe in order to receive Dharma teachings and to realize them in your mindstream, imagine the entire universe and everything beautiful in it, and respectfully offer it to the field of merit.

This ground, anointed with perfume, flowers strewn,
Mount Meru, four lands, sun and moon,
Imagined as a Buddha land and offered to you.
May all beings enjoy this pure land.

The objects of attachment, aversion, and ignorance – friends, enemies, and strangers, my body, wealth, and enjoyments – I offer these without any sense of loss. Please accept them with pleasure, and inspire me and others to be free from the three poisonous attitudes.

Idam guru ratna mandala kam nirya tayami

All the beings in the field of merit receive your offerings with delight. The offerings dissolve into light and absorb into the Buddha's heart. From his heart, light radiates to you, filling your body and mind, and inspiring you to accomplish the path.

Requesting Inspiration

To progress on the path and develop the realizations of the path to awakening, you need the inspiration of the lineage of spiritual mentors, especially your principal teacher or root guru, the one who touched your heart so deeply with the Dharma. Thus request:

Glorious and precious root guru, sit upon the lotus and moon seat on my crown. Guiding me with your great kindness, bestow upon me the attainments of your body, speech, and mind.

A replica of your teacher, in the aspect of the Buddha, emerges from the Buddha in front of you and comes to sit on a lotus and moon cushion on your head, facing the same direction as you. The Buddha on your crown acts as an advocate for you in requesting inspiration from the entire field of merit as you make request to the lineage teachers:

Buddha, unequalled teacher and guide; Venerable protector Maitreya, his successor; Superior Asanga, prophesied by Buddha; to you three Buddhas and bodhisattvas I make request.

Buddha, head of the Shakya clan, the foremost guide, peerless in expounding emptiness; Manjushri, embodiment of the Buddha's complete wisdom; exalted Nagarjuna, best of the Superiors who sees the profound meaning; to you three crowning jewels of clear exposition I make request.

Atisha, upholder of this great vehicle, who sees the profundity of dependent arising; Drom Rinpoche, elucidator of this good path; to these two ornaments of the world I make request.

Avalokiteshvara, great treasure of objectless compassion; Manjushri, master of flawless wisdom; Tsongkhapa, crown jewel of the Snowy Land's sages, Lobsang Drakpa, I make request at your feet.

Holder of the white lotus, embodiment of all the conquerors' compassion, guide benefiting migrating beings in the land of snow mountains and beyond, sole deity and refuge, Tenzin Gyatso, at your feet, I make request.

The eyes through whom the vast scriptures are seen, supreme doors for the fortunate who would cross over to spiritual freedom, illuminators whose wise means vibrate with compassion, to the entire line of spiritual mentors I make request.

(Optional: Review the stages of the path by reciting "The Foundation of All Good Qualities," "The Three Principal Aspects of the Path," or "The Thirty-Seven Practices of Bodhisattvas.")

All the figures in the field of merit melt into light and dissolve into the central figure of the Buddha in front of you. As the embodiment of the Three Jewels, the Buddha now absorbs into the Buddha on your crown. As you recite the Buddha's mantra, much white light flows from the Buddha into you, purifying all negativities and obscurations and generating within you all the realizations of the stages of the path.

Tayata om muni muni maha muniye soha (at least 21x)

Meditation on the Stages of the Path

Now do one of the analytical meditations of the stages of the path.

Absorption

At the conclusion of your meditation, the Buddha on your head melts into light and dissolves into you.[6] Your body, speech, and mind become inseparable from those of the Buddha. (Meditate)

Dedication

> *Due to this merit may we soon*
> *Attain the awakened state of Guru Buddha,*
> *That we may be able to liberate*
> *All sentient beings from their sufferings.*
>
> *May the precious bodhi mind*
> *Not yet born arise and grow.*
> *May that born have no decline,*
> *But increase forever more.*

Abbreviated Recitations

Refuge

Namo Gurubhya.
Namo Buddhaya.
Namo Dharmaya.
Namo Sanghaya. (3x or 7x)

Refuge and Bodhicitta

I take refuge until I have awakened in the Buddhas, the Dharma and the Sangha. By the merit I create by engaging in generosity and the other far-reaching practices, may I attain Buddhahood in order to benefit all sentient beings. (3x)

The Four Immeasurables

May all sentient beings have happiness and its causes.
May all sentient beings be free of suffering and its causes.
May all sentient beings not be separated from sorrowless bliss.
May all sentient beings abide in equanimity, free of bias, attachment and anger.

Seven Limb Prayer

Reverently I prostrate with my body, speech and mind,
And present clouds of every type of offering, actual and mentally transformed.
I confess all my destructive actions accumulated since beginningless time,
And rejoice in the virtues of all holy and ordinary beings.

Please remain until cyclic existence ends,
And turn the wheel of Dharma for sentient beings.
I dedicate all the virtues of myself and others to the great
awakening.

Mandala Offering

This ground, anointed with perfume, flowers strewn,
Mount Meru, four lands, sun and moon,
Imagined as a Buddha land and offered to you.
May all beings enjoy this pure land.

The objects of attachment, aversion and ignorance – friends,
enemies and strangers, my body, wealth and enjoyments – I offer
these without any sense of loss. Please accept them with pleasure,
and inspire me and others to be free from the three poisonous
attitudes.

Idam guru ratna mandala kam nirya tayami

Requesting Inspiration

Glorious and precious root guru, sit upon the lotus and moon seat
on my crown. Guiding me with your great kindness, bestow upon
me the attainments of your body, speech and mind.

The eyes through whom the vast scriptures are seen, supreme doors
for the fortunate who would cross over to spiritual freedom,
illuminators whose wise means vibrate with compassion, to the
entire line of spiritual mentors I make request.

Shakyamuni Buddha's Mantra

Tayata om muni muni maha muniye soha   (21x)

Dedication of Merit

Due to this merit may we soon
Attain the awakened state of Guru Buddha,
That we may be able to liberate
All sentient beings from their sufferings.

May the precious bodhi mind
Not yet born arise and grow.
May that born have no decline,
But increase forever more.

Short Texts to Recite and Contemplate

The Three Principal Aspects of the Path

I bow down to the venerable spiritual mentors.

I will explain, as well as I am able, the essence of all the teachings of the Conqueror, the path praised by the Conquerors and their spiritual children, the entrance for the fortunate ones who desire liberation.

Listen with clear minds, you fortunate ones who direct your minds to the path pleasing to the Buddha and strive to make good use of freedom and fortune without being attached to the joys of cyclic existence.

For you embodied beings bound by the craving for existence, without the pure determination to be free (renunciation) from the ocean of existence, there is no way for you to pacify the attractions to its pleasurable effects. Thus, from the outset seek to generate the determination to be free.

By contemplating the freedoms and fortunes so difficult to find and the fleeting nature of your life, reverse the clinging to this life. By repeatedly contemplating the infallible effects of karma and the miseries of cyclic existence, reverse the clinging to future lives.

By contemplating in this way, do not generate even for an instant the wish for the pleasures of cyclic existence. When you have, day and night unceasingly, the mind aspiring for liberation, you have generated the determination to be free.

However, if your determination to be free is not sustained by the pure altruistic intention (bodhicitta), it does not become the cause for the perfect bliss of unsurpassed awakening. Therefore, the intelligent generate the supreme thought of awakening.

Swept by the current of the four powerful rivers[7], tied by the strong bonds of karma which are so hard to undo, caught in the iron net of self-grasping egoism, completely enveloped by the darkness of ignorance,

Born and reborn in boundless cyclic existence, unceasingly tormented by the three sufferings[8] – by thinking of all mother sentient beings in this condition, generate the supreme altruistic intention.

Even if you meditate upon the determination to be free and the altruistic intention, without the wisdom realizing the ultimate nature, you cannot cut the root of cyclic existence. Therefore, strive for the means to realize dependent arising.

One who sees the infallible cause and effect of all phenomena in cyclic existence and beyond and destroys all false perceptions (of their inherent existence) has entered the path which pleases the Buddha.

Appearances are infallible dependent arisings; emptiness is free of assertions (of inherent existence or non-existence). As long as these two understandings are seen as separate, one has not yet realized the intent of the Buddha.

When these two realizations are simultaneous and concurrent, from the mere sight of infallible dependent arising comes definite knowledge which completely destroys all modes of mental grasping. At that time, the analysis of the profound view is complete.

In addition, appearances clear away the extreme of (inherent) existence; emptiness clears away the extreme of non-existence. When you understand the arising of cause and effect from the viewpoint of emptiness, you are not captivated by either extreme view.

In this way, when you have realized the exact points of the three principal aspects of the path, by depending on solitude, generate the power of joyous effort and quickly accomplish the final goal, my spiritual child!

By Je Tsongkhapa

A Song of the Four Mindfulnesses[9]

On the unwavering cushion of the union of method and wisdom
Sits the kind Lama who is the nature of all protectors.
There is a Buddha in the state of culmination of realizations and cessations.
Beseech him in the light of admiration, through casting away critical thoughts.
Don't let your mind go astray, but place it within admiration and reverence.
Through not losing mindfulness, hold it within admiration and reverence.

In unending samsara, the prison of suffering,
Wander the sentient beings of the six realms, bereft of happiness.
They are your parents, who reared you with affectionate kindness.
Meditate on compassion and affection by relinquishing attachment and aversion.
Don't let your mind go astray, but place it within compassion.
Through not losing mindfulness, hold it within compassion.

In the celestial mansion of great bliss, joyous to sustain,
There exists the divine form of your body which is a purified state of the aggregates.
There is a deity in the nature of union of the three divine bodies.
Don't view it as ordinary, but train in divine dignity and immaculate appearance.
Don't let your mind go astray, but place it within profundity and clarity.
Through not losing mindfulness, hold it in an attitude of profundity and luminosity.

The sphere of appearing and existing phenomena
Is pervaded by the space of the ultimate clear light of suchness.
There is an ineffable ultimate reality.
View this nature of emptiness through abandoning mental contrivances.
Don't let your mind go astray, but place it in the ambiance of reality.
Through not losing mindfulness, hold it in the ambiance of reality.

At the crossroads of the six collections (of consciousness) which have diverse perceptions,
Are seen the hazy dualistic phenomena which are baseless.
There is a magical show which is by nature deceptive.
Don't believe it to be true, but view it as having the nature of emptiness.
Don't let your mind go astray, but place it in the nature of appearance-emptiness.
Through not losing mindfulness, hold it in the nature of appearance-emptiness.

By H.H. Kalsang Gyatso, Dalai Lama VII, translated by Geshe Dorji Damdul

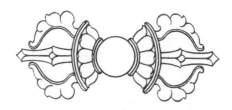

Eight Verses of Thought Transformation

1. With the thought of attaining awakening
   For the welfare of all beings,
   Who are more precious than a wish-fulfilling jewel,
   I will constantly practice holding them dear.

2. Whenever I am with others
   I will practice seeing myself as the lowest of all,
   And from the very depths of my heart
   I will respectfully hold others as supreme.

3. In all actions I will examine my mind
   And the moment a disturbing attitude arises,
   Endangering myself and others,
   I will firmly confront and avert it.

4. Whenever I meet a person of bad nature
   Who is overwhelmed by destructive energy and intense
   suffering,
   I will hold such a rare one dear,
   As if I had found a precious treasure.

5. When others, out of jealousy,
   Mistreat me with abuse, slander and so on,
   I will practice accepting defeat
   And offering the victory to them.

6. When someone I have benefited
   And in whom I have placed great trust
   Hurts me very badly,
   I will practice seeing that person as my supreme teacher.

7. In short, I will offer directly and indirectly
   Every benefit and happiness to all beings, my mothers.
   I will practice in secret taking upon myself
   All their harmful actions and sufferings.

8. Without these practices being defiled by the stains of the eight
   worldly concerns
   And by perceiving all phenomena as illusory,
   I will practice without grasping to release all beings
   From the bondage of the disturbing unsubdued mind and
   karma.

By Langri Thangpa

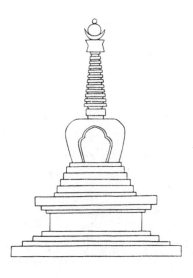

The Thirty-Seven Practices of Bodhisattvas

1. Having gained this rare ship of freedom and fortune,
   Hear, think and meditate unwaveringly night and day
   In order to free yourself and others
   From the ocean of cyclic existence –
   This is the practice of bodhisattvas.

2. Attached to your loved ones you're stirred up like water.
   Hating your enemies you burn like fire.
   In the darkness of confusion you forget what to adopt and
   discard.
   Give up your homeland –
   This is the practice of bodhisattvas.

3. By avoiding bad objects, disturbing emotions gradually
   decrease.
   Without distraction, virtuous activities naturally increase.
   With clarity of mind, conviction in the teaching arises.
   Cultivate seclusion –
   This is the practice of bodhisattvas.

4. Loved ones who have long kept company will part.
   Wealth created with difficulty will be left behind.
   Consciousness, the guest, will leave the guest-house of the body.
   Let go of this life –
   This is the practice of bodhisattvas.

5. When you keep their company your three poisons increase,
   Your activities of hearing, thinking, and meditating decline,
   And they make you lose your love and compassion.
   Give up bad friends –
   This is the practice of bodhisattvas.

6. When you rely on them your faults come to an end
   And your good qualities grow like the waxing moon.
   Cherish spiritual teachers
   Even more than your own body –
   This is the practice of bodhisattvas.

7. Bound himself in the jail of cyclic existence,
   What worldly god can give you protection?
   Therefore when you seek refuge, take refuge in
   The Three Jewels that will not betray you –
   This is the practice of bodhisattvas.

8. The Subduer said all the unbearable suffering
   Of bad rebirths is the fruit of wrong-doing.
   Therefore, even at the cost of your life,
   Never do wrong –
   This is the practice of bodhisattvas.

9. Like the dew on the tip of a blade of grass, pleasures of the three
   worlds
   Last only a while and then vanish.
   Aspire to the never-changing
   Supreme state of liberation –
   This is the practice of bodhisattvas.

10. When your mothers, who've loved you since time without
    beginning,
    Are suffering, what use is your own happiness?
    Therefore to free limitless living beings
    Develop the altruistic intention –
    This is the practice of bodhisattvas.

11. All suffering comes from the wish for your own happiness.
    Perfect Buddhas are born from the thought to help others.
    Therefore exchange your own happiness
    For the suffering of others –
    This is the practice of bodhisattvas.

12. Even if someone out of strong desire
    Steals all your wealth or has it stolen,
    Dedicate to him your body, possessions
    And your virtue, past, present and future –
    This is the practice of bodhisattvas.

13. Even if someone tries to cut off your head
    When you haven't done the slightest thing wrong,
    Out of compassion take all her misdeeds
    Upon yourself –
    This is the practice of bodhisattvas.

14. Even if someone broadcasts all kinds of unpleasant remarks
    About you throughout the three thousand worlds,
    In return, with a loving mind,
    Speak of his good qualities –
    This is the practice of bodhisattvas.

15. Though someone may deride and speak bad words
    About you in a public gathering,
    Looking on her as a spiritual teacher,
    Bow to her with respect –
    This is the practice of bodhisattvas.

16. Even if a person for whom you've cared
    Like your own child regards you as an enemy,
    Cherish him specially, like a mother
    Does her child who is stricken by sickness –
    This is the practice of bodhisattvas.

17. If an equal or inferior person
    Disparages you out of pride,
    Place her, as you would your spiritual teacher,
    With respect on the crown of your head –
    This is the practice of bodhisattvas.

18. Though you lack what you need and are constantly disparaged,
    Afflicted by dangerous sickness and spirits,
    Without discouragement take on the misdeeds
    And the pain of all living beings –
    This is the practice of bodhisattvas.

19. Though you become famous and many bow to you,
    And you gain riches equal to Vaishravana's,
    See that worldly fortune is without essence,
    And be unconceited –
    This is the practice of bodhisattvas.

20. While the enemy of your own anger is unsubdued,
    Though you conquer external foes, they will only increase.
    Therefore with the militia of love and compassion
    Subdue your own mind –
    This is the practice of bodhisattvas.

21. Sensual pleasures are like saltwater:
    The more you indulge, the more thirst increases.
    Abandon at once those things which breed
    Clinging attachment –
    This is the practice of bodhisattvas.

22. Whatever appears is your own mind.
    Your mind from the start was free from fabricated extremes.
    Understanding this, do not take to mind
    [Inherent] signs of subject and object –
    This is the practice of bodhisattvas.

23. When you encounter attractive objects,
    Though they seem beautiful
    Like a rainbow in summer, don't regard them as real
    And give up attachment –
    This is the practice of bodhisattvas.

24. All forms of suffering are like a child's death in a dream.
    Holding illusory appearances to be true makes you weary.
    Therefore when you meet with disagreeable circumstances,
    See them as illusory –
    This is the practice of bodhisattvas.

25. When those who want awakening must give even their body,
    There's no need to mention external things.
    Therefore without hope for return or any fruition
    Give generously –
    This is the practice of bodhisattvas.

26. Without ethical conduct you can't accomplish your own well-
    being,
    So wanting to accomplish others' is laughable.
    Therefore without worldly aspirations
    Safeguard your ethical conduct –
    This is the practice of bodhisattvas.

27. To Bodhisattvas who want a wealth of virtue
    Those who harm are like a precious treasure.
    Therefore towards all cultivate fortitude
    Without hostility –
    This is the practice of bodhisattvas.

28. Seeing even Hearers and Solitary Realizers, who accomplish
    Only their own good, strive as if to put out a fire on their head,
    For the sake of all beings make enthusiastic effort,
    The source of all good qualities –
    This is the practice of bodhisattvas.

29. Understanding that disturbing emotions are destroyed
    By insight with serenity,
    Cultivate concentration which surpasses
    The four formless absorptions –
    This is the practice of bodhisattvas.

30. Since the five perfections without wisdom
    Cannot bring perfect awakening,
    Along with skillful means cultivate the wisdom
    Which does not conceive the three spheres [as real] –
    This is the practice of bodhisattvas.

31. If you don't examine your own errors,
    You may look like a practitioner but not act as one.
    Therefore, always examining your own errors,
    Rid yourself of them –
    This is the practice of bodhisattvas.

32. If through the influence of disturbing emotions
    You point out the faults of another Bodhisattva,
    You yourself are diminished, so don't mention the faults
    Of those who have entered the Great Vehicle –
    This is the practice of bodhisattvas.

33. Reward and respect cause us to quarrel
    And make hearing, thinking and meditating decline.
    For this reason give up attachment to
    The households of friends, relations, and benefactors –
    This is the practice of bodhisattvas.

34. Harsh words disturb the minds of others
    And cause deterioration in the bodhisattva's conduct.
    Therefore give up harsh words
    Which are unpleasant to others –
    This is the practice of bodhisattvas

35. Habitual disturbing emotions are hard to stop through
    counteractions.
    Armed with antidotes, the guards of mindfulness and mental
    alertness
    Destroy disturbing emotions like attachment
    At once, as soon as they arise –
    This is the practice of bodhisattvas.

36. In brief, whatever you are doing,
    Ask yourself, "What's the state of my mind?"
    With constant mindfulness and mental alertness
    Accomplish others' good –
    This is the practice of bodhisattvas.

37. To remove the suffering of limitless beings,
    Understanding the purity of the three spheres,
    Dedicate the virtue from making such effort
    To awakening –
    This is the practice of bodhisattvas.

By Gyalse Togmay Zangpo, translated by Ruth Sonam

The Foundation of All Good Qualities

The kind and venerable spiritual mentor is the foundation of all good qualities. Seeing that dependence on him or her is the root of the path, I request inspiration to rely on him or her with great respect and continuous effort.

A human life with leisure is obtained this once. Understanding that it has great value and is hard to find, I request inspiration to generate unceasingly the mind that takes hold of its essence day and night.

The fluctuation of our body and life is like a bubble of water; remember death, for we perish so quickly. After death, the effects of black and white karma pursue us as a shadow follows a body. Finding certainty in this, I request inspiration to always be careful to abandon even the slightest destructive action and to complete the accumulation of virtue.

There is no satisfaction in enjoying worldly pleasures. They are the door to all misery. Having realized that the fault of samsaric perfections is that they cannot be trusted, I request inspiration to be strongly intent on the bliss of liberation.

That pure thought (to attain liberation) produces great conscientiousness, mindfulness, and awareness. I request inspiration to make the essential practice keeping the vows of individual liberation, the root of the doctrine.

Having seen that all beings, my kind mothers, have fallen like me into the ocean of cyclic existence, I request inspiration to train in the supreme altruistic intention, assuming the responsibility to free all migrating beings.

Generating the altruistic intention alone, without cultivation of the three ethical practices,[10] does not lead to awakening. Having realized this, I request inspiration to practice with intense effort the vows of the conquerors and their spiritual children.

By quieting distraction to false objects,[11] and analyzing the meaning of reality, I request inspiration to generate quickly within my mind stream the path uniting serenity and insight.

When, trained in the common path,[12] I am a suitable vessel, I request inspiration to enter with ease the great gateway of the fortunate ones, the Vajrayana,[13] the supreme of all vehicles.

The basis of achieving the two powerful attainments is the pure vows and commitments that I have pledged. Having found true understanding of this, I request inspiration to keep them even at the cost of my life.

Having realized the significance of the two stages,[14] which are the essence of the tantric path, I request inspiration to steadfastly practice without laziness the four sessions of yoga, and realize what the holy beings have taught.

May the spiritual teachers who lead me on the sacred path and all spiritual friends who practice it have long life. Please inspire me to quickly and completely pacify all outer and inner hindrances.

In all my rebirths may I never be separated from perfect spiritual mentors, and enjoy the magnificent Dharma. Completing all qualities of the stages and paths, may I quickly achieve the stage of Vajradhara.

By Je Tsongkhapa

Je Tsongkhapa

The Extensive Offering Practice

Preliminaries

Make offerings on your altar. Do "Meditation on the Buddha" or "Je Tsongkhapa Guru Yoga," inserting the extensive offering practice just before the offering verse.

Generate Bodhicitta

To attain awakening in order to benefit all my kind mother sentient beings, I will make these extensive offerings to all sentient beings and then, together we will make offerings to the spiritual mentors and the Three Jewels. By this may all of us become fully awakened Buddhas.

Purify the Place and Invite the Merit Field to Come

Everywhere may the ground be pure, free of the roughness of pebbles and so forth. May it be the nature of lapis and as smooth as the palm of one's hand.

Imagine the Buddha or Je Tsongkhapa as the central figure in the field of merit. He is surrounded by all the Buddhas and bodhisattvas. All of them are emanations of the transcendental wisdom of bliss and emptiness and are the nature of your root spiritual mentor and the deity. They have the same essence of blissful, compassionate wisdom, but are given different labels because they appear in different forms. Invite them to come:

Protector of all beings without exception, divine subduer of innumerable destructive forces, deity, perfect knower of all things, Bhagavan and attendants, please come here.

You appear as the deity in the nature of great bliss non-dual with emptiness. Think that each offering – water bowls, flowers, incense, lights, perfume, food, music, and so forth, actual offering substances as well as those you visualize – is in the nature of great bliss non-dual with emptiness. By thinking that the nature of the offerings is great bliss, it is easy to feel that they generate infinite bliss in the holy minds of each figure in the field of merit. You also create more merit by offering pure substances.

Consecrate the offerings on the altar as well as other offerings such as flower gardens, forests, parks, lakes, meadows, and lights, candlelight, electric lights, and the light of the sun and moon and transform them into the nature of great bliss and emptiness by contemplating:

May offering substances human and divine, those actual and those which are emanated, unsurpassed Samantabhadra clouds of offerings fill the entire space.

om namo bhagavate bendzay sarwaparma dana tathagataya arhate samyaksam buddhaya tayata om bendzay bendzay maha bendzay maha taydza bendzay maha bidya bendzay maha bodhicitta bendzay maha bodhi mendo pasam kramana bendzay sarwa karma awarana bisho dana bendzay soha

By the power of the truth of the Three Jewels, the power of the blessings of all the Buddhas and bodhisattvas, the power of the great might of the completed two collections, and the power of the intrinsically pure and inconceivable sphere of reality, may (these offerings) become suchness.

Offering to Sentient Beings

Make charity of all these offerings to sentient beings. Give them to each hell being, hungry ghost, animal, human being, demi-god, god, intermediate state being, arhat, and bodhisattva. In this way, the people who are starving, homeless, unable to find a job or have a very hard life receive these offerings. This eliminates their suffering and now all of you together will make offerings to the Three Jewels.

Sentient beings experience difficulties because they lack merit, which they need to be successful and happy. By thinking that we give sentient beings things to offer to the Three Jewels and by making offerings on their behalf, we create merit and dedicate it for their benefit.

Offering to the Three Jewels

Put your palms together so that you bow to the spiritual mentors and the Three Jewels while making offerings to them. Think that each holy being is the manifestation of your spiritual mentor and the deity that you practice. Also imagine a complete field of merit exists in each pore of each figure in the field of merit.

Visualize the countless Buddhas in the ten directions receiving clouds of offerings. Offer the offerings placed on your altar as well as skies filled with beautiful offerings. Think that you generate infinite bliss in their holy minds by making these offerings.

Offer these extensive offerings to all your spiritual mentors and to all the holy objects in this country, and generate great bliss in their holy minds. Visualize giving them these spectacular offerings many times.

Next offer all these nectars, flowers, lights and so forth to His Holiness the Dalai Lama, other spiritual mentors in India, and to all the holy objects in India, including in Bodgaya where 1000 Buddhas will descend. Offer to them many times.

Offer to all the holy beings and holy objects in Tibet, including the Shakyamuni Buddha statue in the Lhasa Temple. Remember to think of them as the nature of great bliss and emptiness, the nature of your root spiritual mentor and the deity. Offer to them many times, generating great bliss in their minds.

Make offerings to your spiritual mentors, holy beings, and holy objects in Nepal, especially the most precious stupa at Bodhanath and in all other Buddhist countries: China, Taiwan, Thailand, Sri Lanka, Burma, Japan and so forth.

Offer to your spiritual mentors, holy beings, and holy objects in Western countries and in the rest of the world.

Make offerings to each and every Buddha, bodhisattva, arhat, statue, stupa, and scripture in this universe and beyond. The more people make images of the Buddha, the more merit you will create by making offerings to the Three Jewels they represent. Offer as many times as possible by thinking of them as the nature of great bliss and emptiness, and generate infinite bliss in their holy minds while reciting the offering verses 1, 3, or 7 times:

These actually performed and mentally imagined water bowl offerings, the manifestations of my innate wisdom awareness, these clouds of offerings equaling the infinite sky, I offer to all my spiritual mentors and the Three Jewels, and to the statues, stupas, and scriptures, which are their manifestations.

Due to this merit, may whomever I promised to pray for and whoever prays for me – principally friends, benefactors and disciples – as well as all sentient beings living and dead, may the rays of the light of the five wisdoms completely purify all their degenerated vows and commitments right now. May they soon actualize the meaning of the Dharma in their minds.

May the sufferings of the lower realms cease right now. May the three realms of samsara be empty right now. May all impure minds be purified of obscurations. May all appearances be purified. May the five holy bodies and wisdom spontaneously arise.

Dedication

Complete "Meditation on the Buddha" or "Je Tsongkhapa Guru Yoga," and then dedicate:

Due to having made these extensive offerings to all holy beings and holy objects, may I, my family members, and all the students and benefactors, especially those who dedicate their lives for others and those who offer service at this abbey, monastery, or Dharma center, and all other sentient beings be able to actualize completely the pure teachings of the Buddha. May we live in pure ethical conduct and courageously engage in extensive bodhisattva deeds and the yoga of the two stages, in order to actualize the transcendental wisdom of non-dual bliss and emptiness.

Composed by Zopa Rinpoche, edited by Thubten Chodron. Printed with permission from Lama Yeshe Wisdom Archives.

Evening Chants

Paying Homage and Bowing to the Buddha

Na Mo Ben Shi Tsay Tya Mu Ni Fo
(Homage to the fundamental teacher, Shakyamuni Buddha)

Praise to Amitabha Buddha

Amitabha's body is the color of gold.
The splendor of his hallmarks has no peer.
The light of his brow shines around a hundred worlds.
Wide as the seas are his eyes pure and clear.
Shining in his brilliance by transformation are countless
Bodhisattvas and infinite Buddhas.
His 48 vows will be our liberation. In nine lotus stages we reach
the farthest shore.

Homage to the Buddha of the Western Pure Land, kind and
compassionate Amitabha. (3x)

Namo Amitabha (repeatedly)

Refuge and Dedication

I take refuge in the Buddha. May all sentient beings understand the
Great Way profoundly and bring forth the bodhi mind.

I take refuge in the Dharma. May all sentient beings deeply enter
the sutra treasury and have wisdom vast as the sea.

I take refuge in the Sangha. May all sentient beings form together
a great assembly, one and all in harmony.

Purification Practices

There are a variety of purification practices, "The Bodhisattva's Confession of Ethical Downfalls" being one of the most popular. This text is also called "The Sutra of the Three Heaps" because the prose text after the names of the thirty-five Buddhas deals with three important topics: confession of downfalls, rejoicing at our own and others' virtues, and dedication of merit. We all have done actions that we now feel badly about doing, and we have aspects of ourselves that we do not like and wish to change. Purification practices are excellent means to remove emotional burdens such as guilt, as well as to pacify the obstacles to our happiness and self-improvement created by the imprints of our destructive actions. Guilt over past actions is useless, only leaving us feeling helpless and hopeless. On the other hand, acting to purify the destructive imprints and afflictions is very productive. It helps us to change our bad habits, and subdues obstacles to long life and success in our spiritual practice.

A complete purification practice consists of four opponent powers:

1. The power of regret for having done the destructive action.

2. The power of reliance: taking refuge, which restores our relationship with holy objects, and generating the altruistic intention, which restores our relationship with other sentient beings.

3. The power of the remedial action, e.g. prostration, offering, reciting the names of the Buddha, reading or contemplating the Dharma, etc.

4.   The power of the promise not to repeat the action.

These four opponent powers are found in "The Bodhisattva's Confession of Ethical Downfalls," the Vajrasattva meditation, and other practices.

There are several visualizations of the thirty-five Buddhas. The easiest is to visualize Shakyamuni Buddha, golden in color, with thirty-four light rays coming from his heart. These light rays form five rows and upon each ray is seated a Buddha. The Buddhas in each row resemble one of the five Dhyani Buddhas.

In the first row are the next six Buddhas mentioned in the prayer. They resemble Akshobya Buddha, blue, the left hand in his lap in the gesture of meditative equipoise, the right hand in the earth-touching gesture (on the right knee, palm down). However, the One Thus Gone, the King with Power over the Nagas, looks slightly different: he has a blue body, a white face, and his hands are folded together at his heart.

In the second row, the next seven Buddhas resemble Vairocana Buddha, white, with both hands at the heart, the index fingers extended.

In the third row, the next seven Buddhas resemble Ratnasambhava Buddha, yellow. His left hand is in meditative equipoise, and his right hand is in the gesture of giving (on the right knee, palm outwards).

In the fourth row, the next seven Buddhas resemble Amitabha Buddha, red, with both hands in meditative equipoise on his lap.

In the fifth row, the next seven Buddhas resemble Amogasiddhi Buddha, green. The left hand is in meditative equipoise and the right hand is bent at the elbow, the palm facing outwards.

Visualize that you are surrounded by all sentient beings in human form and that you are leading them in prostrating to the Buddhas. While prostrating, imagine much light coming from the Buddhas and flowing into you and into all the sentient beings around you. This light purifies all imprints of destructive actions and all afflictions.

After reciting the names of the thirty-five Buddhas and the prayer of the three heaps – confession, rejoicing, and dedication – you may also want to recite the "General Confession."

After this, visualize the thirty-four Buddhas dissolve into Shakyamuni Buddha. He comes on top of your head and melts into golden light. The light descends through the crown of your head and goes to your heart chakra, in the center of your chest. Feel that all destructive karma and obscurations have been completely purified and that your mind has become inseparable from the Buddha's pure mind of wisdom and compassion.

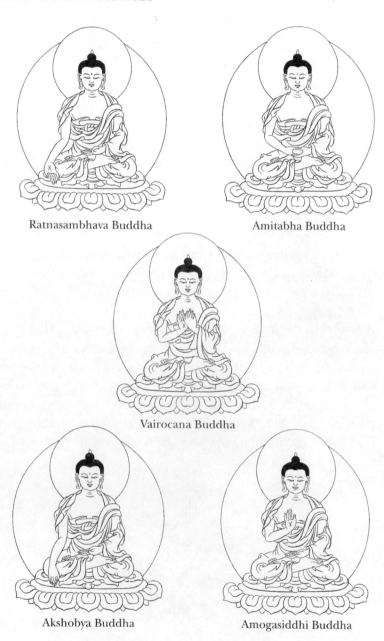

Ratnasambhava Buddha

Amitabha Buddha

Vairocana Buddha

Akshobya Buddha

Amogasiddhi Buddha

The Five Dhyani Buddhas

The Bodhisattvas' Confession
of Ethical Downfalls
Prostrations to the Thirty-Five Buddhas

To increase the benefit of each prostration, first prostrate three times while reciting:

om namo manjushriye namo sushriye namo uttama shriye soha.

Continue to prostrate while reciting the names of the Buddhas and the confession prayer.

I, (say your name) throughout all times, take refuge in the Gurus; I take refuge in the Buddhas; I take refuge in the Dharma; I take refuge in the Sangha.

To the Founder, the Transcendent Destroyer, the One Thus Gone,[15] the Foe Destroyer, the Fully Awakened One, the Glorious Conqueror from the Shakyas, I bow down.
To the One Thus Gone, the Great Destroyer, Destroying with Vajra Essence, I bow down.
To the One Thus Gone, the Jewel Radiating Light, I bow down.
To the One Thus Gone, the King with Power over the Nagas, I bow down.
To the One Thus Gone, the Leader of the Warriors, I bow down.
To the One Thus Gone, the Glorious Blissful One, I bow down.
To the One Thus Gone, the Jewel Fire, I bow down.

To the One Thus Gone, the Jewel Moonlight, I bow down.
To the One Thus Gone, Whose Pure Vision Brings Accomplishments, I bow down.
To the One Thus Gone, the Jewel Moon, I bow down.
To the One Thus Gone, the Stainless One, I bow down.
To the One Thus Gone, the Glorious Giver, I bow down.
To the One Thus Gone, the Pure One, I bow down.
To the One Thus Gone, the Bestower of Purity, I bow down.

To the One Thus Gone, the Celestial Waters, I bow down.
To the One Thus Gone, the Deity of the Celestial Waters, I bow down.
To the One Thus Gone, the Glorious Good, I bow down.
To the One Thus Gone, the Glorious Sandalwood, I bow down.
To the One Thus Gone, the One of Unlimited Splendor, I bow down.
To the One Thus Gone, the Glorious Light, I bow down.
To the One Thus Gone, the Glorious One without Sorrow, I bow down.

To the One Thus Gone, the Son of the Desireless One, I bow down.
To the One Thus Gone, the Glorious Flower, I bow down.
To the One Thus Gone, Who Understands Reality Enjoying the Radiant Light of Purity, I bow down.
To the One Thus Gone, Who Understands Reality Enjoying the Radiant Light of the Lotus, I bow down.
To the One Thus Gone, the Glorious Gem, I bow down.
To the One Thus Gone, the Glorious One who is Mindful, I bow down.
To the One Thus Gone, the Glorious One whose Name is Extremely Renowned, I bow down.

To the One Thus Gone, the King Holding the Banner of Victory over the Senses, I bow down.

To the One Thus Gone, the Glorious One who Subdues Everything Completely, I bow down.

To the One Thus Gone, the Victorious One in All Battles, I bow down.

To the One Thus Gone, the Glorious One Gone to Perfect Self-control, I bow down.

To the One Thus Gone, the Glorious One who Enhances and Illuminates Completely, I bow down.

To the One Thus Gone, the Jewel Lotus who Subdues All, I bow down.

To the One Thus Gone, the Foe Destroyer, the Fully Awakened One, the King with Power over Mount Meru, always remaining in the Jewel and the Lotus, I bow down.

(Optional: If you wish to bow to the seven Medicine Buddhas)

To the Buddha, Renowned Glorious King of Excellent Signs, I bow down.

To the Buddha, King of Melodious Sound, I bow down.

To the Buddha, Stainless Excellent Gold, I bow down.

To the Buddha, Supreme Glory Free From Sorrow, I bow down.

To the Buddha, Melodious Ocean of Renowned Dharma, I bow down.

To the Buddha, Delightful King of Clear Knowing, I bow down.

To the Medicine Buddha, King of Lapis Light, I bow down.

All you thirty-five Buddhas, and all the others, those thus gone, foe destroyers, fully awakened ones and transcendent destroyers who are existing, sustaining and living throughout the ten directions of sentient beings' worlds – all you Buddhas, please give me your attention.

In this life, and throughout beginningless lives in all the realms of samsara, I have created, caused others to create, and rejoiced at the creation of destructive karmas such as misusing offerings to holy objects, misusing offerings to the Sangha, stealing the possessions of the Sangha of the ten directions; I have caused others to create these destructive actions and rejoiced at their creation.

I have created the five heinous actions,[16] caused others to create them and rejoiced at their creation. I have committed the ten non-virtuous actions,[17] involved others in them, and rejoiced in their involvement.

Being obscured by all this karma, I have created the cause for myself and other sentient beings to be reborn in the hells, as animals, as hungry ghosts, in irreligious places, amongst barbarians, as long-lived gods, with imperfect senses, holding wrong views, and being displeased with the presence of a Buddha.

Now before these Buddhas, transcendent destroyers who have become transcendental wisdom, who have become the compassionate eye, who have become witnesses, who have become valid and see with their omniscient minds, I am confessing and accepting all these actions as destructive. I will not conceal or hide them, and from now on, I will refrain from committing these destructive actions.

Buddhas and transcendent destroyers, please give me your attention: in this life and throughout beginningless lives in all the realms of samsara, whatever root of virtue I have created through even the smallest acts of charity such as giving one mouthful of food to a being born as an animal, whatever root of virtue I have created by keeping pure ethical conduct, whatever root of virtue I have created by abiding in pure conduct, whatever root of virtue I have created by fully ripening sentient beings' minds, whatever root of virtue I have created by generating bodhicitta, whatever root of virtue I have created of the highest transcendental wisdom.

Bringing together all these merits of both myself and others, I now dedicate them to the highest of which there is no higher, to that even above the highest, to the highest of the high, to the higher of the high. Thus I dedicate them completely to the highest, fully accomplished awakening.

Just as the Buddhas and transcendent destroyers of the past have dedicated, just as the Buddhas and transcendent destroyers of the future will dedicate, and just as the Buddhas and transcendent destroyers of the present are dedicating, in the same way I make this dedication.

I confess all my destructive actions separately and rejoice in all merits. I implore all the Buddhas to grant my request that I may realize the ultimate, sublime, highest transcendental wisdom.

To the sublime kings of the human beings living now, to those of the past, and to those who have yet to appear, to all those whose knowledge is as vast as an infinite ocean, with my hands folded in respect, I go for refuge.

General Confession

Woe is me!

O spiritual mentors, great vajra holders, and all the Buddhas and bodhisattvas who abide in the ten directions, as well as all the venerable Sangha, please pay attention to me.

I, who am named _____, circling in cyclic existence since beginningless time until the present, overpowered by afflictions such as attachment, hostility, and ignorance, have created the ten destructive actions by means of body, speech and mind. I have engaged in the five heinous actions and the five parallel heinous actions.[18] I have transgressed the precepts of individual liberation,[19] contradicted the trainings of a bodhisattva,[20] broken the tantric commitments.[21] I have been disrespectful to my kind parents, spiritual mentors, spiritual friends, and those following the pure paths. I have committed actions harmful to the Three Jewels, avoided the holy Dharma, criticized the Arya[22] Sangha, and harmed living beings. These and many other destructive actions I have done, have caused others to do, and have rejoiced in others' doing. In short, I have created many obstacles to my own higher rebirth and liberation, and have planted countless seeds for further wanderings in cyclic existence and miserable states of being.

Now in the presence of the spiritual mentors, the great vajra holders, all the Buddhas and bodhisattvas who abide in the ten directions, and the venerable Sangha, I confess all of these destructive actions, I will not conceal them and I accept them as destructive. I promise to refrain from doing these actions again in the future. By confessing and acknowledging them, I will attain and abide in happiness, while by not confessing and acknowledging them, true happiness will not come.

Dedication Verses

Selected Dedication Verses

Dedication of merit prevents the merit from being damaged by anger or wrong views and ensures it will ripen in the way you wish. Dedicate the merit created by yourself and others in the past, present, and future.

Due to this merit may we soon
Attain the awakened state of guru-Buddha,
That we may be able to liberate
All sentient beings from their sufferings.

May the precious bodhi mind
Not yet born arise and grow.
May that born have no decline,
But increase forever more.

May anyone who merely sees, hears, remembers, touches or talks to me be freed in that very instant from all sufferings and abide in happiness forever.

In all my rebirths may I never be separated from perfect spiritual mentors and enjoy the magnificent Dharma. Completing all qualities of the stages and paths, may I quickly attain the state of Vajradhara.[23]

Without harming them, may I always stop all beings in all worlds who wish to commit harmful deeds.

Since it is due to my teacher's kindness that I have met the Buddha's peerless teaching, I dedicate this virtue so that all beings may be guided by sublime spiritual mentors.

Until cyclic existence ends, may the teaching of this Beneficent One be unshaken by the wind of superstitions. May the world be filled with those who find conviction in the Teacher by understanding the teaching's true nature.

Throughout all my births, even when giving away my body and life, may I never fail to uphold for even an instant the excellent way of the Sage, which illumines the principle of dependent arising.

Day and night, may I pass the time thinking and examining by what means these teachings can be spread in the minds of myself and others.

In order to train like the hero Manjushri who knows reality as it is and just like Samantabhadra as well, I completely dedicate all this goodness just as they did.

With that dedication which is praised as greatest by all the Buddhas gone to freedom in the three times, I too dedicate all my roots of goodness for the attainments of the bodhisattva practice.

May sentient beings, who have all been my mother and father, be completely happy, and may the lower realms be forever empty. May all the prayers of bodhisattvas, in whatever places they live, be immediately fulfilled.

May I experience whatever sufferings sentient beings have, and may they experience whatever happiness and virtue I have.

May the glorious spiritual mentors live long, and may all beings throughout limitless space have happiness. By purifying our defilements and accumulating merit, may I and all others be inspired to attain Buddhahood quickly.

May I never develop for even a moment wrong views towards the deeds of my glorious spiritual mentors. By seeing whatever actions they do as pure, with respect and devotion, may the spiritual mentors' inspiration flow into my mind.

In all my lives, through the Victorious One, Je Tsongkhapa, acting as my Mahayana spiritual mentor, may I never turn away for even an instant from the excellent path praised by the Victorious Ones.

May I and others be able to live in pure ethical conduct, train our minds in bodhicitta, and develop pure view and conduct. In this way, may we complete our lives without corrupting the pure wisdom of Je Tsongkhapa, (who is like) the second Buddha.

Dedication from the
Stages of the Path to Awakening

By accumulating through long effort, the two collections as vast as the sky, may I become the chief of the Victorious Ones, a guide of all beings whose minds are blinded by ignorance.

In all lives until I reach that point, may Manjushri look after me with loving-kindness. After I find the supreme path, complete in the stages of the teaching, my I please all the Victorious Ones by accomplishing it.

By skillful means inspired by strong loving-kindness, may the vital points of the path that I precisely know clear away the mental darkness of beings. May I then uphold the Victorious One's teachings for a long time.

In regions where the supreme, precious teaching has not spread or where it has spread but then declined, with my heart deeply moved by great compassion, may I illuminate this treasure of happiness and benefit.

May the stages of the path to awakening, well-founded on the wondrous deeds of the Buddhas and bodhisattvas, bring glory to the minds of those who seek freedom and long preserve the Victorious One's achievements.

May all human and non-human beings who eliminate adversity and provide conducive conditions for practicing the excellent path never be parted in any of their lives from the pure path praised by the Buddhas.

When we strive to properly accomplish the Universal Vehicle through the ten deeds of the teaching, may we always be assisted by the mighty ones and may oceans of good fortune spread everywhere.

By Je Tsongkhapa

Dedication Verses from
Engaging in the Deeds of Bodhisattvas

May all beings everywhere
Plagued by sufferings of body and mind
Obtain an ocean of happiness and joy
By virtue of my merits.

May no living creature suffer,
Commit evil or ever fall ill.
May no one be afraid or belittled,
With a mind weighed down by depression.

May the blind see forms,
And the deaf hear sounds.
May those whose bodies are worn with toil
Be restored on finding repose.

May the naked find clothing,
The hungry find food.
May the thirsty find water
And other delicious drinks.

May the poor find wealth,
Those weak with sorrow find joy.
May the forlorn find hope,
Constant happiness and prosperity.

May all who are ill and injured
Quickly be freed from their ailments.
Whatever diseases there are in the world,
May these never occur again.

May the frightened cease to be afraid
And those bound be freed.
May the powerless find power
And may people think of benefiting each other.

For as long as space endures
And as long as living beings remain,
Until then may I too abide
To dispel the misery of the world.

By Shantideva

Dedication for a Meaningful Life

Whatever actions I do – eating, walking, sitting, sleeping, working, and so forth – and whatever I experience in life – up or down, happiness or pain, healthy or sick, harmony or discord, success or failure, wealth or poverty, praise or criticism – whether I am living or dying, or even born in a horrible rebirth; whether I live long or not – may my life be beneficial for all sentient beings. The main purpose of my life is not simply to be rich, respected, famous, healthy, and happy. The meaning of my life is to benefit all sentient beings. Therefore, from now on, may whatever actions I do be beneficial for all beings. May whatever I experience in life – happiness or suffering – be dedicated to actualizing the path to awakening. May whatever I do, say, or think benefit all sentient beings and help them to attain full awakening quickly.

By Kyabje Zopa Rinpoche, lightly edited by Ven. Chodron

Long Life Prayers

Long Life Prayer for His Holiness the Dalai Lama

In the snowy mountain pure land
You're the source of good and happiness.
Powerful Tenzin Gyatso Chenresig,
May you stay until samsara ends.

Long Life Prayer for All Spiritual Mentors

May the spiritual mentors [teachers] who lead me on the sacred path and all spiritual friends who practice it have long life. May I pacify completely all outer and inner hindrances – grant such inspiration, I pray.

May the lives of the venerable spiritual mentors be stable, and their virtuous actions spread in the ten directions. May the light of Lobsang's teachings, dispelling the darkness of the beings in the three worlds, always increase.

Ven. Thubten Chodron's Long Life Prayer
by Tsenzhap Serkong Rinpoche

Peerless supreme spiritual leader, omniscient King of the Shakyas, Motherly Tara, supreme bestower of longevity and wisdom, vast ocean assembly of sources of Refuge, grant propitiousness here and now for a nectar of benefit and bliss to flow.

With a clear mind of extensive learning gained from following the wondrous traditions of Thubten – the Able One's teachings – you bring clarity to masses of disciples with the light of Chodron – the lamp of the Dharma. May your lotus-feet remain unfaltering for a very long time.

Through your Dharmic deeds of hearing, thinking, meditating and so on, place those who seek the liberated path in harmony through immaculate discipline. Please lead all beings to liberation with undeclining excellent qualities of scripture and insight, and establish them in a glory of eternal bliss.

Prayer for Sravasti Abbey
by Tsenzhap Serkong Rinpoche

May the deeds of explaining and practicing the Dharma done by groups supporting the teachings and their upholders, who spread the view of dependent arising and non-violent actions in the ten directions – and especially at Sravasti Abbey in the West – flourish.

Request to Je Tsongkhapa

Avalokiteshvara, great treasure of objectless compassion,
Manjushri, master of flawless wisdom,
Vajrapani, destroyer of all demonic forces
Tsongkhapa, crown jewel of the Snowy Lands' sages
Lobsang Drakpa, I make request at your holy feet. (3x)

Mig may tse way ter chen chen re sig
Dri may kyen pay wong po jam pel yang
Du pung ma lu jom dze sang way dag
Gang chen kay pay tsug kyen tsong kha pa
Lo sang drag pay zhab la sol wa deb (3x)

Verses Before and After Meals

Five Contemplations Before Meals[24]

1. I contemplate all the causes and conditions and the kindness of others by which I received this food.
2. I contemplate my own practice, constantly trying to improve it.
3. I contemplate my mind, cautiously guarding it from wrongdoing, greed, and other defilements.
4. I contemplate this food, treating it as wondrous medicine to nourish my body.
5. I contemplate the aim of Buddhahood, accepting and consuming this food in order to accomplish it.

Offering Verses Before Eating

Imagine the food as blissful wisdom nectar inside a vast jeweled vessel, and recite, "om ah hum" three times to consecrate the food. Offer it to a small Buddha visualized at your heart chakra.

Great compassionate Protector,
All-knowing Teacher,
Field of merit and good qualities vast as an ocean –
To the Tathagata, I bow.

Through purity, freeing from attachment,
Through virtue, freeing from the lower realms,
Unique, supreme ultimate reality –
To the Dharma that is peace, I bow.

Having freed themselves, showing the path to freedom too,
Well established in the trainings,
The holy field endowed with good qualities –
To the Sangha, I bow.

To the supreme teacher, the precious Buddha,
To the supreme refuge, the holy precious Dharma,
To the supreme guides, the precious Sangha,
To all the objects of refuge we make this offering.

May we and all those around us never be separated from the Triple Gem in any of our lives. May we always have the opportunity to make offerings to them. And may we continually receive their blessings and inspiration to progress along the path.

By seeing this food as medicine, I will consume it without attachment or hatred, not to increase my arrogance, strength, or good looks, but solely to sustain my life.

As you eat, imagine that Shakyamuni Buddha at your heart experiences bliss. He radiates light that fills your entire body.

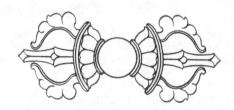

Verses After Lunch

om utsita bandi ashibya soha (to offer to the pretas)
tayata gate gate paragate parasamgate bodhi soha

chomdenday deshin shegpa drachompa yangdagpar tsogpay
sangye rinchen okyi gyalpo may o rabtu selwa la chag tsal lo (3x)

nama samanta prabhara jaya tathagataya arhate samyaksam
buddhaya namo manjushriye kumara bhutaya bodhisattvaya
mahasattvaya maha karunikaya tayata om niralambha nirabhase
jaya jaye lambhe mahamate daki dakenam meparishvadha soha
(3x)

May all those who offered me food attain happiness of total peace. May all those who offered me drink, who served me, who received me, who honored me, or who made offerings to me attain happiness which is total peace.

May all those who scold me, make me unhappy, hit me, attack me with weapons, or do things up to the point of killing me attain the happiness of awakening. May they fully awaken to the unsurpassed, perfectly accomplished state of Buddhahood.

By the merit of offering food, may they have a good complexion, magnificence, and strength. May they find foods having hundreds of tastes and live with the food of samadhi.

By the merit of offering drink, may their afflictions, hunger, and thirst be pacified. May they possess good qualities such as generosity and take a rebirth without any sickness or thirst.

The one who gives, the one who receives, and the generous action are not to be observed as truly existent. By giving with impartiality, may the benefactors attain perfection.

By the power of being generous, may they become Buddhas for the benefit of sentient beings, and through generosity, may all the beings who have not been liberated by previous conquerors be liberated.

By the merit of this generosity, may the naga kings, gods having faith in the Dharma, leaders who support religious freedom, benefactors, and others living in the area live long, enjoy good health and prosperity, and attain lasting happiness.

Due to this virtue, may all beings complete the collections of merit and wisdom. May they attain the two Buddha bodies resulting from merit and wisdom.

Verses for Various Occasions

Monastic Mind Motivation

Having a "monastic mind" benefits our Dharma practice whether we are monastics or lay practitioners. A monastic mind is one that is humble, imbued with the Buddhist worldview, dedicated to cultivating mindfulness, clear knowing, love, compassion, wisdom, and other good qualities. Being mindful of the kindness I have received from all sentient beings, I will relate to them with patience, kindness, and compassion. I will be mindful of my precepts and values and will cultivate clear knowing of my thoughts and feelings, as well as how I speak and act. I will take care to act and speak at suitable times and in appropriate ways, abandoning idle talk and disruptive movements. With respect for others and confidence in my good qualities, I will be humble and easy for others to speak to. In all these activities, I will endeavor to remember impermanence and the emptiness of inherent existence and to act with bodhicitta.

Offering Service[25]

We are grateful for the opportunity to offer service to the Buddha, Dharma, and Sangha and to sentient beings. While working with others, differences in ideas and ways of doing things may arise. These are natural and are a source of creative exchange; our minds don't need to make them into conflicts. We will endeavor to listen deeply and communicate wisely and kindly as we work together for our common goal. By using our body and speech to support the values we deeply believe in – generosity, kindness, ethical conduct, love, and compassion – we will create great merit which we dedicate for the awakening of all beings.

Offering Food to the Sangha

With a mind that takes delight in giving, I offer these requisites to the Sangha and the community. Through my offering, may they have the food they need to sustain their Dharma practice. They are genuine Dharma friends who encourage, support and inspire me along the path. May they become realized practitioners and skilled teachers who will guide us on the path. I rejoice at creating great merit by offering to those intent on virtue and dedicate this for the awakening of all sentient beings. Through my generosity, may we all have conducive circumstances to develop heartfelt love, compassion, and altruism for each other and to realize the ultimate nature of reality.

Sangha Receives the Food

Your generosity is inspiring and we are humbled by your faith in the Three Jewels. We will endeavor to keep our precepts as best as we can, to live simply, to cultivate equanimity, love, compassion, and joy, and to realize the ultimate nature so that we can repay your kindness in sustaining our lives. Although we are not perfect, we will do our best to be worthy of your offering. Together, we will create peace in a chaotic world.

Preparing Food

We are going to offer service by preparing a meal for the community of Dharma practitioners. How fortunate we are to have the opportunity to prepare and cook this food. The food will nourish their bodies and the love we put into preparing it will nourish their hearts.

Preparing food is an expression of our kind heart. When we chop, mix and cook, we will work with mindfulness and a relaxed mind. We will leave aside idle talk, and speak with gentle and low voices. The menu will be simple and healthy, free from the distraction of elaborate and complicated menus.

We will wash the veggies and fruits well, thinking that we are cleansing defilements from the minds of sentient beings with the nectar of wisdom. Out of consideration for those who will clean up after the meal, we will tidy up after ourselves. Let's take joy in working harmoniously together for the benefit of all!

Verses by Bhikshuni Thubten Chodron

First Pg 2s

The Eight Mahayana Precepts Ceremony

Introduction

The eight Mahayana precepts are taken for twenty-four hours. It is especially good to take them on full and new moon days and on other Buddhist festival days. Observing precepts for even such a short time has tremendous benefits: one accumulates a great amount of merit in a short time. One will receive upper rebirths and eventually will attain awakening. One is protected from harm and the place where one lives becomes peaceful and prosperous. One's mind is peaceful and calm; one gains control over one's bad habits; there are fewer distractions when meditating. One gets along better with others. One will meet the Buddha's teachings in the future and can be born as a disciple of Maitreya Buddha.

The eight precepts are:

1. Avoid killing, directly or indirectly.
2. Avoid stealing and taking things without the permission of their owner.
3. Avoid sexual contact.
4. Avoid lying and deceiving others.
5. Avoid intoxicants: alcohol, tobacco and recreational drugs (you may take prescription drugs).
6. Avoid eating more than one meal that day. The meal is taken before noon, and once one has stopped eating for thirty minutes, the meal is considered finished. At other times of the day one can take light drinks, but not undiluted whole milk or fruit juice with pulp. Avoid eating meat, chicken, fish, eggs, onions, garlic, and radishes.

7. Avoid sitting on a high, expensive bed or seat with pride. Also avoid sitting on animal skins.
8. Avoid wearing jewelry, perfume, and make-up. Avoid singing, dancing or playing music with attachment.

For a precept to be broken completely, four conditions must be present:

1. The motivation is a destructive attitude such as attachment, anger, etc.
2. There is an object of the action, e.g. a being that is killed or an object that is stolen.
3. One does the action. If one tells someone else to kill, steal or lie, it is also a transgression.
4. The action is completed, e.g. the being dies before oneself or one thinks, "This is mine."

The first time one takes the precepts, it is done from a spiritual mentor. Thereafter, one can do the ceremony before a Buddha image by regarding it as the actual Buddha.

Preliminary Prayers

First recite the Abbreviated Recitations (page 28) through the Mandala Offering. Then generate a strong wish to attain awakening for the benefit of all sentient beings. With that motivation, kneel on your right knee and take the precepts.

Taking the Precepts

All Buddhas and bodhisattvas residing in the ten directions, please pay attention to me!
Preceptor, please pay attention to me! (omit if taking before a Buddha image.)

Just as the past tathagatas, the foe destroyers and the completely perfect Buddhas, like the heavenly steed and the great elephant, accomplished their objective and did their task, laid down their load (of the contaminated aggregates), achieved their own purpose, consumed their ties to samsara; as they possessed perfect speech, a mind properly liberated, a wisdom properly liberated; just as they perfectly took the Mahayana precepts for the sake of all sentient beings, to benefit them, to liberate them, to eliminate famine, to eliminate sickness, to perfect the thirty-seven aids to awakening, and to realize the highest perfect awakening; in the same way, for the sake of all sentient beings, to benefit them, to liberate them, to eliminate famine, to eliminate sickness, to perfect the thirty-seven aids to awakening, and to realize the highest perfect awakening, I, (say your name), will also perfectly accept the Mahayana precepts from this moment until sunrise tomorrow. (3x)

Prayer of commitment to keep the precepts

From now on I will not kill, or take another's property. I will not engage in sexual activity and will not speak false words. I will totally avoid intoxicants, which are the cause of many faults. I will not use high or expensive beds or seats. I will avoid eating food at improper times. I will not wear perfumes, garlands and ornaments, or sing, dance and so forth. Just as the foe destroyers abandoned killing and so forth, may I, by avoiding killing and so forth, quickly attain the highest awakening. May all beings be freed from the ocean of cyclic existence, this world disturbed by many sorrows.

Dharani of Pure Ethical Conduct

om ahmoga shila sambara bara bara maha shuda sato payma bibu kitay budza dara dara samanta ahwalokite hum pey soha (21x)

Dedication Verses

By having the flawless ethical conduct of the Dharma, pure ethical conduct, and ethical conduct without conceit, may I complete far-reaching ethical conduct. *At end then Pg 66 dedication verses*

Follow this by reciting other dedication prayers. *Pg 69*

Refuge and Precepts

This ceremony is a good way for lay practitioners to purify and restore their precepts. It is good to do on full and new moon days, or twice monthly on any days that you can.

Purification Verse

Every harmful action I have done
With my body, speech, and mind
Overwhelmed by attachment, anger, and confusion,
All these I openly lay bare before you. (3x)

Renewing Refuge and Precepts

Spiritual mentors, Buddhas and bodhisattvas who abide throughout infinite space, please pay attention to me. From beginningless time until the present, in my attempt to find happiness, I have been taking refuge; but the things I have relied upon have not been able to bring the lasting state of peace and joy that I seek. Until now, I have taken refuge in material possessions, money, status, reputation, approval, praise, food, sex, music and a myriad of other things. Although these things have given me some temporal pleasure, they lack the ability to bring me lasting happiness because they themselves are transient and do not last long. My attachment to these things has in fact made me more dissatisfied, anxious, confused, frustrated and fearful.

Seeing the faults of expecting more from these things than they can give me, I now turn for refuge to a reliable source that will never disappoint me: the Buddhas, the Dharma and the Sangha. I take refuge in the Buddhas as the ones who have done what in the depth of my heart I aspire to do – purified their minds of all defilements and brought to fulfillment all their positive qualities. I take refuge in the Dharma, the cessation of all undesirable experiences and their causes and the path leading to that state of peace. I take refuge in the Sangha, those who have directly realized reality and who want to help me do the same.

I take refuge not only in the "outer" Three Jewels – those beings who are Buddhas or Sangha and the Dharma in their mindstreams – but I also take refuge in the "inner" Three Jewels – the Buddha, Dharma and Sangha that I will become in the future. Because I have the Buddha potential within me at this very moment and will always have this potential as an inseparable part of my mind, the outer Three Jewels will act as the cause for me to be transformed into the resultant inner Three Jewels.

The Three Jewels are my real friends that will always be there and will never let me down. Being free of all judgment and expectations, they only wish me well and continually look upon me and all beings with the eyes of kindness, acceptance and understanding. By turning to them for refuge, may I fulfill all wishes of myself and all beings for good rebirths, liberation and full awakening.

Just as a sick person relies on a wise doctor to prescribe medicine and on nurses to help them, I as a person suffering from the constantly recurring ills of cyclic existence, now turn to the Buddha, a skillful doctor who prescribes the medicine of the Dharma – ethical conduct, concentration, wisdom, altruism, and the path of Tantra. The Sangha act as nurses who encourage me and show me how to take the medicine. However, being surrounded by the best doctor, medicine and nurses will not cure the illness; the patient must actually follow the doctor's advice and take the medicine. Similarly, I need to follow the Buddha's guidelines and put the teachings into practice as best as I can. The

Buddha's first advice, the first medicine to take to soothe my ills, is to train myself in the five precepts.

Therefore, with a joyful heart that seeks happiness for myself and others, today I will commit myself to follow some or all of those precepts.

1. From my own experience and examination, I know that harming others, specifically taking their lives, harms myself and others. Therefore, I undertake to protect life and to avoid killing. By my doing this, all beings will feel safe around me and peace in the world will be enhanced.

2. From my own experience and examination, I know that taking things that have not been given to me harms myself and others. Therefore, I undertake to respect and protect others' property and to avoid stealing or taking what has not been freely given. By my doing this, all beings can be secure around me and harmony and generosity in society will increase.

3. From my own experience and examination, I know that engaging in unwise sexual behavior harms myself and others. Therefore, I undertake to respect my own and others' bodies, to use my sexuality wisely and kindly, and to avoid sexual expression which could harm others or myself physically or mentally. By my doing this, all beings will be able to relate to me honestly and with trust, and mutual respect among people will ensue.

4. From my own experience and examination, I know that saying untrue things for the sake of personal gain harms myself and others. Therefore, I undertake to speak truthfully and to avoid lying or deceiving others. By my doing this, all beings can trust my words and friendship among people will increase.

5. From my own experience and examination, I know that taking intoxicants harms myself and others. Therefore, I undertake to avoid taking intoxicating substances – alcohol, recreational drugs and tobacco – and to keep my body and environment clean. By my doing this, my mindfulness and introspective alertness will increase, my mind will be clearer, and my actions will be thoughtful and considerate.

Having previously wandered in confusion and used misdirected methods in an attempt to be happy, today I am delighted to choose to live in accord with these wise guidelines of the Buddha. Remembering that the Buddhas, bodhisattvas and arhats – those beings I admire so much – have also followed these guidelines, I too will enter the path to liberation and awakening just as they have done.

May all beings throughout infinite space reap the benefits of my living in accord with the precepts! May I become a fully awakened Buddha for the benefit of all!

By Bhikshuni Thubten Chodron

Guidelines for the Practice of Refuge

Having taken refuge, a safe and sound direction, in the Three Jewels – Buddha, Dharma, and Sangha – it is advantageous to follow certain guidelines for practice in order to make progress along the path to awakening.

1. In analogy to taking refuge in the Buddha, commit yourself whole-heartedly to a qualified spiritual mentor.

2. In analogy to taking refuge in the Dharma, listen to and study the teachings as well as put them into practice in your daily life.

3. In analogy to taking refuge in the Sangha, respect the Sangha as your spiritual companions and follow the good examples they set.

4. Avoid being rough and arrogant, running after any desirable object you see and criticizing anything that meets with your disapproval.

5. Be friendly and kind to others and be concerned more with correcting your own faults than with pointing out those of others.

6. As much as possible avoid the ten non-virtuous actions, and take and keep precepts.[26]

7. Have a compassionate and sympathetic heart towards all other sentient beings.

8. Make special offerings to the Three Jewels on Buddhist festival days.

Guidelines in terms of each of the Three Jewels

1. Having taken refuge in the Buddha, who has purified all defilements and developed all excellent qualities, do not turn for refuge to worldly deities, who lack the capacity to guide you from all problems.

Respect all images of the Buddha: do not put them in low or dirty places, step over them, point your feet towards them, sell them to earn a living or use them as collateral. When looking at various images, do not discriminate, "This Buddha is beautiful, but this one is not." Do not treat with respect expensive and impressive statues while neglecting those that are damaged or less costly.

2. Having taken refuge in the Dharma, avoid harming any living being.

Also, respect the written words which describe the path to awakening by keeping the texts clean and in a high place. Avoid stepping over them, putting them on the floor, or throwing them in the rubbish when they are old. It is best to burn or recycle old Dharma materials.

3. Having taken refuge in the Sangha, do not cultivate the friendship of people who criticize the Buddha, Dharma, and Sangha or who have unruly behavior or do many harmful actions. By becoming friendly with such people, you may be influenced in the wrong way by them. However, that does not mean you should criticize or not have compassion for them.

Also, respect monks and nuns as they are people who are making earnest efforts to actualize the teachings. Respecting them helps your mind, for you appreciate their qualities and are open to learn from their example. By respecting even the robes of ordained beings, you will be happy and inspired when seeing them.

Common guidelines

1. Mindful of the qualities, skills, and differences between the Three Jewels and other possible refuges, repeatedly take refuge in the Buddha, Dharma and Sangha.

2. Remembering their kindness, make offerings to them, especially offering your food before eating. (See the prayers for this.)

3. Mindful of their compassion, encourage others to take refuge in the Three Jewels.

4. Remembering the benefits of taking refuge, do so three times in the morning and three times in the evening, by reciting and reflecting upon any of the refuge prayers.

5. Do all actions by entrusting yourself to the Three Jewels.

6. Do not forsake your refuge at the cost of our life, or even as a joke.

The Six Preparatory Practices

Prior to the first meditation session of the day, it is good to do the six preparatory practices:

1. Sweep and clean the room and arrange the altar.

2. Make offerings on the altar, e.g. light, food, incense, water bowls, etc.

3. Sit in a comfortable position and examine your mind. Do breathing meditation to calm your mind. Then establish a good motivation. After that, take refuge and generate the altruistic intention by reciting the appropriate prayers.

4. Visualize the merit field with the spiritual mentors, Buddhas, bodhisattvas, and so forth. If this is too difficult, visualize Shakyamuni Buddha and consider him the embodiment of all Buddhas, Dharma and Sangha.

5. Offer the seven limb prayer and the mandala, by reciting those prayers.

6. Make requests to the lineage spiritual mentors for inspiration by reciting the requesting prayers.

Then do one of the meditations on the stages of the path to awakening.

Practicing Dharma in Daily Life

Waking Up

In the morning when you wake up, visualize the Buddha on the
crown of your head and think, "How fortunate I am that so far I
have not died. Again today I have the opportunity to practice the
Dharma. I again have the opportunity to take the essence of this
precious human life that has so many freedoms and fortunes. This
great essence is to practice bodhicitta, the mind that is dedicated to
attaining awakening for the benefit of all sentient beings, and to do
this by giving up my self-centeredness and by cherishing others.
Self-preoccupation is the greatest obstacle to being happy myself
and to bringing about the happiness of all sentient beings. So from
now on, I will never allow myself to be under the control of the
self-centered thought.

"Cherishing others is the best means to be happy and successful
myself and especially to bring about the happiness desired by all
sentient beings. Therefore, from now on, I will never separate
from the precious bodhicitta – the loving, compassionate mind that
cherishes other sentient beings – for even one moment. I will live
my life with kindness, love, compassion, and bodhicitta."

Then make a sincere request to the Buddha, "Whether I experience
happiness or pain, may whatever actions I do with my body,
speech and mind always become only the cause to quickly lead
mother sentient beings throughout infinite space to awakening."

Guru Shakyamuni Buddha is extremely pleased with your request.
He melts into light, which flows down through your crown to your
heart, inspiring and transforming your mind. Think, "I have
received all of the Buddha's qualities – serenity, love, compassion,

altruism, friendliness, kindness, wisdom and other wonderful qualities." Imagine a small Buddha made of light appears at your heart. Throughout the day, think of the Buddha constantly. In this way, you will become more mindful of what you do, say and think, as you will be aware of the Buddha witnessing it.

Contemplate the "Eight Verses of Thought Transformation" (see page 36)

By remembering Guru Shakyamuni Buddha, do your daily life actions as follows:

Eating and Drinking

Before you eat or drink, think, "I am going to make this food (drink) offering to Guru Shakyamuni Buddha, who is the embodiment of all the Buddhas, Dharma, and Sangha, in order to attain full awakening for the sake of all mother sentient beings." Think the food is very pure like sweet nectar that gives great bliss and tastes delicious, similar to what the Buddha experiences. This food is completely beyond the usual ordinary appearance of food. Offer the food with the verses in this book, and imagine that the Buddha at your heart experiences bliss as you eat.

Enjoying Sense Objects

Whatever sense objects you enjoy during the day – clothes, music, beautiful scenery and so forth – think that you are offering them to Guru Shakyamuni Buddha who is at your heart. In this way, you continuously make offerings to the Buddha, thus creating a great collection of merit. Also, you will become less attached to sense pleasures and will begin to enjoy them with a peaceful mind.

Making Offerings on the Altar

Think, "I am going to make these offerings in order to attain awakening for the benefit of all suffering mother sentient beings who have been kind to me since beginningless rebirths." Consecrate the food, flowers, water, light and so forth that you offer by saying, "OM AH HUM" three times.

When you look at the pictures and statues of the Buddhas and holy beings on your altar, think that they are all the spiritual mentors, Buddhas, Dharma and Sangha of the ten directions. Offer to them with this recognition, and imagine that they generate great bliss by receiving your offerings. Offer to the statues of the Buddhas and deities (which represent Buddha's holy body), to all the scriptures (which represent the Buddha's holy speech), and to all the stupas (which represent the Buddha's holy mind) that exist throughout the universe. This is the most skillful way to accumulate merit. In this way, you make offerings to each and every holy object without needing to take even one step or spend even one dollar to travel to those places. By thinking that all the statues, Buddhas, bodhisattvas and so forth are manifestations of the guru, you accumulate the highest merit.

After offering, think, "Whatever happiness and virtue I have created, may all sentient beings receive it, and whatever suffering sentient beings have, may it ripen upon me." Then dedicate the merit.

Working

When you go to work, think, "I must achieve awakening in order to lead each and every sentient being to awakening. Therefore, I am going to offer service for sentient beings by going to work.

May whoever comes in contact with the results of my work have a peaceful mind and generate bodhicitta."

While you are at work, remember the kindness of the other sentient beings who gave you the job and who make it possible for you to earn a living. Thinking in this way helps to avoid generating destructive emotions such as anger at work.

Bathing

Think, "I am going to transform bathing into the cause to attain awakening for the benefit of all sentient beings." By thinking in a new way, make your shower or bath a purification practice. One way to think is that the water is very blissful and you are offering it to the Buddha at your heart. Another way is to visualize whichever manifestation of the Buddha you feel a strong connection with (for example, Chenresig or Tara) above your head and think that the bathing water is flowing from his/her hand. The water is the nature of wisdom, and it is making your mind clear so you can practice the path for the benefit of sentient beings. While you are washing, think that all destructive karmas, sicknesses and interfering forces are washed away by the wisdom realizing emptiness and that you receive all the realizations and qualities of the Buddha.

Preparing for Bed

At the end of the day it is important to purify any destructive actions created during the day. The most powerful method to do this is by means of the four opponent powers:

1. Having regret for the destructive actions you have done.
2. Taking refuge and generating bodhicitta.

3. Doing remedial actions, for example bowing to the 35 Buddhas.
4. Determining not to do the action again in the future.

Doing these four stops the karmas from multiplying each day, each week, each month. It also purifies the destructive karma accumulated since beginningless time. By cleansing these obstacles, you will have the opportunity to become a Buddha.

Before going to bed, think, "I take refuge until I have awakened in the Buddhas, the Dharma and the Sangha. By the merit I create by engaging in generosity and the other far-reaching practices, may I attain Buddhahood in order to benefit all sentient beings."

Visualize Guru Vajrasattva on your crown. Light and nectar flow down from his heart into you and purify all destructive karmas and obscurations of yourself and others. While visualizing this, recite Vajrasattva's mantra:

Om vajrasattva hum (28x)

Then Vajrasattva says to you, "All of your destructive karmas and obscurations are completely purified. Feel delighted." Vajrasattva absorbs to your heart and inspires your mind.

May the precious bodhi mind
Not yet born arise and grow.
May that born have no decline,
But increase forever more.

In all my lives, with the Victorious One, Je Tsongkhapa, acting as the actual Mahayana spiritual mentor, may I never turn aside for even an instant from the excellent path praised by the Victorious Ones.

Due to the merit accumulated by myself and others in the past, present and future, may anyone who merely sees, hears, remembers, touches or talks to me be freed in that very instant from all sufferings and abide in happiness forever.

When you go to bed, think, "I am going to practice sleeping yoga in order to become a Buddha for the benefit of all sentient beings." Lie down in the lion position, which is how Buddha laid when he passed away: lie on your right side, with your right hand under your cheek. Your left hand is on your left thigh, and your legs are extended. Remember the kindness and sufferings of sentient beings and go to sleep feeling love and compassion towards them. Visualize Guru Shakyamuni Buddha on your pillow, and put your head in his lap. Very gentle light flows from the Buddha into you, and while remembering the Buddha's awakened qualities with devotion, fall asleep.

By Kyabje Zopa Rinpoche

Praise of the Teacher, the Buddha, Through His Twelve Deeds

By skillful compassion born in the Shakya clan,
You vanquished Mara's forces while others could not,
Your body radiant like a mountain of gold,
King of the Shakyas – homage at your feet.

You first produced the thought of bodhi,
Then completed the two collections of merit and wisdom
To become the protector of sentient beings
Through your vast deeds in this age, I praise.

You benefited the gods, then knowing it was time
To tame others too, you descended from the celestial realm
As an elephant, saw the clan of your birth,
And entered the womb of Queen Maya – homage to this deed.

When ten months had passed, you were born
Shakya Prince in fortunate Lumbini Grove;
Brahma and Indra praised you with your supreme marks
And confirmed your bodhi-lineage – homage to this deed.

As a powerful youth, lion amongst humans,
You showed skill in Anga and Magadha,
Vanquished all people inflated with arrogance,
Unrivaled one – homage to this deed.

By skillful means, to conform to the conduct of the world
And to avert any censure,
You governed a kingdom and assumed a retinue
And queen – homage to this deed!

Seeing samsaric activities have no essence,
You left the householder's life and went forth,
And became fully renounced
At the stupa of great purity – homage to this deed.

You practiced austerities for six years
On the banks of the Nairanjana River,
Diligently intent on awakening and perfect in effort,
Attained the supreme meditative stability – homage to this deed.

To bring to fruition the efforts you made
From beginningless time,
Unmoving, you sat beneath the bodhi tree in Magadha
And fully awakened to perfect bodhi – homage to this deed.

Swiftly observing beings with compassion,
In Varanasi and other holy places
You turned the Wheel of Dharma, setting disciples
On the three vehicles – homage to this deed.

You vanquished the maras in the land of Kormojik
And put an end to the erroneous wrangling
Of Devadatta, the six heretical teachers, and others,
Sage victorious! Homage to this deed.

With qualities unmatched in the three worlds,
At Sravasti you displayed wondrous miracles,
And spread the teachings; devas and humans
Made great offerings to you – homage to this deed.

To exhort the lazy to practice the Dharma,
At the pure site Kushinagar,
You manifested the perishing of the deathless, vajra-like body
And entered nirvana – homage to this deed.

Because in reality there is no destruction
And so future sentient beings could create merits
At that very place you left many relics –
The eight portions of your remains – homage to this deed.

By the Teacher's coming to the world,
By his doctrine's brilliance, like sunlight,
By harmony among the doctrine's holders,
Long may the Dharma abide – may all be auspicious.

Consecration Ritual

A Ritual Inviting the Awakened Ones to Abide in an Object or Place of Worship

Refuge and Bodhicitta

I take refuge until I have awakened in the Buddhas, the Dharma and the Sangha. By the merit I create by engaging in generosity and the other far-reaching practices, may I attain Buddhahood in order to benefit all sentient beings. (3x)

Invocation

All you Buddhas and bodhisattvas abiding in the ten directions, please pay attention to me. Until all sentient beings equaling the extent of space are placed in the stage of non-abiding nirvana, may all the Conquerors not pass beyond sorrow but remain firmly. In particular, may the exalted wisdom beings, the Conquerors who arose and are invited in these supports of the holy body, speech and mind, not pass beyond sorrow but remain firmly until the supports are destroyed due to harm by earth, water, fire or wind. Having remained firmly, please bestow upon me and others – all sentient beings – all supreme and ordinary attainments without exception. (3x)

Absorption

Om supratishta vajra ye svaha (3x) (throw rice)

Om ye dharma hetu prabhava hetun teshan tathagato hyavadat teshan chayo nirodha evam vadi maha shramana ye svaha (3x)
(Heart of Dependent Arising Mantra)

Om traiyadha sarva tathagata hridaya garbhe jvala dharmadhatu garbhe samharana ayuhsam shodhaya papam sarva tathagata samanta ushnisha vimale vishuddhe svaha (3x)
(Mantra of Stainless Ushnisha)

Auspicious verses

Like an assortment of many types of jewels set in the mountain of layers of exquisite refined gold, may these supreme holy bodily forms that we can view continuously remain firmly until the end of existence.

May there be the auspiciousness of the immutable glorious holy body,
May there be the auspiciousness of the sixty branches of holy speech,
May there be the auspiciousness of the limitless ultimate holy mind.
May there be the auspiciousness of the Conqueror's holy body, speech and mind.

Notes

[1] "Inspire" or "bless" means to transform our mind. A student has received "blessing" or has been inspired when his/her own mind transforms into the Dharma, i.e. when the student has understood and integrated the meaning of the teachings into his/her life.

[2] Bodhicitta is the aspiration to become a Buddha for the benefit of all sentient beings.

[3] The Buddha's seat represents the three principal realizations of the path: the lotus symbolizes the determination to be free from cyclic existence; the moon represents bodhicitta; the sun is the wisdom realizing emptiness.

[4] The blissful wisdom nectar cures the four maras: afflictions, our polluted aggregates of body and mind, uncontrolled death, and worldly gods who interfere with our practice.

[5] The qualities of the Buddha's body include his ability to transform his body into different forms, animate and inanimate, in order to help sentient beings according to their individual needs and inclinations. With his speech, he can communicate different aspects of the Dharma simultaneously to beings of various levels of development and can be understood by them in their respective languages. His omniscient mind of wisdom and compassion clearly sees everything that exists and knows the thoughts and experiences of every sentient being.

[6] If you have received a full initiation which enables you to visualize yourself as the deity, then instead of visualizing a small Buddha at your heart, you may visualize yourself as the Buddha.

[7] The four rivers are ignorance, sensual desire, craving (for rebirth and self), and wrong views.

[8] The three sufferings (dukkha) are the dukkha of pain, the dukkha of change, and pervasive conditioned dukkha.

[9] Here the four mindfulnesses are the mindfulnesses of the spiritual mentor, compassion, your body as a divine body, and the view of emptiness.

[10] The three ethical practices are restraining from destructive actions, accumulating constructive ones, and working for the benefit of sentient beings.

[11] Objects are false in that their way of appearance and way of existence do not accord, i.e. although objects appear to be inherently existent, in fact they are not; they are empty of inherent existence.

[12] The common path is the general path of the sutrayana (determination to be free, bodhicitta, wisdom realizing emptiness) and the path of the three lower tantras.

¹³ Vajrayana (the tantric path) is a branch of the Mahayana and contains special techniques for transforming one's ordinary body, speech and mind into the body, speech and mind of a Buddha.

¹⁴ The two stages are the generation stage and the completion stage of the highest class of tantra.

¹⁵ The Buddhas are called the Ones Thus Gone (Tathagata) because they have gone beyond the misery of cyclic existence to complete awakening by abandoning all defilements and subtle obscurations. They also have realized the ultimate nature of all phenomena, suchness or emptiness.

¹⁶ The five heinous actions are: causing a schism in the Sangha, killing one's father, killing one's mother, killing an arhat, and drawing blood from the Buddha's body.

¹⁷ The ten non-virtuous actions are: killing, stealing, sexual misconduct, (three of the body); lying, divisive speech, harsh words, idle talk, (four of speech); covetousness, maliciousness, and wrong views (three of mind).

¹⁸ The five parallel heinous actions are: killing a bodhisattva, killing an arya (one who has realized emptiness directly), stealing the provisions or funds of the Sangha community, destroying a monastery or stupa with anger, committing incest with one's mother who is an arhat.

¹⁹ The vows of individual liberation include the five lay precepts, the vows of novice and fully-ordained monks and nuns, and the one-day vows.

²⁰ The trainings of the bodhisattva include the guidelines for aspiring bodhicitta and the 18 root and 46 auxiliary bodhisattva precepts.

²¹ The tantric commitments include the 14 root and 8 auxiliary tantric vows, the 19 samaya of the five Buddha families, and other commitments taken at the time of empowerment into practices of the highest class of tantra.

²² An arya is someone who has realized the emptiness of inherent existence directly and non-conceptually.

²³ Vajradhara is the form that Shakyamuni Buddha appeared in when he taught the tantras. This verse is from "The Foundation of All Good Qualities," the next verse is from Nagarjuna's *Precious Garland*, the four following verses are from Je Tsongkhapa's *Praise to Dependent Arising*, and the two following verses are from the *Flower Ornament Sutra*.

²⁴ The five contemplations are from the Chinese Buddhist tradition.

²⁵ Instead of seeing your job as work, see it as offering service to the Three Jewels and to sentient beings. Recite this verse every day before going to your job.

²⁶ For a lay person, one can take the eight Mahayana precepts for one day, or one can take some or all of the five precepts for the duration of one's life. On the basis of refuge, a lay person may also take bodhisattva precepts and tantric vows.